Coloring Books for Grownups

Day of the Dead Girls

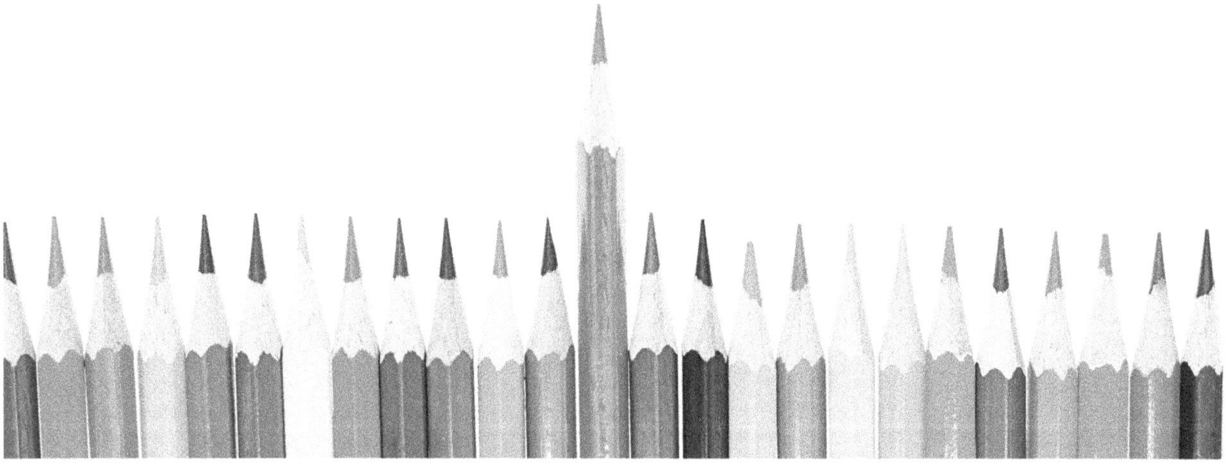

Chiquita publishing

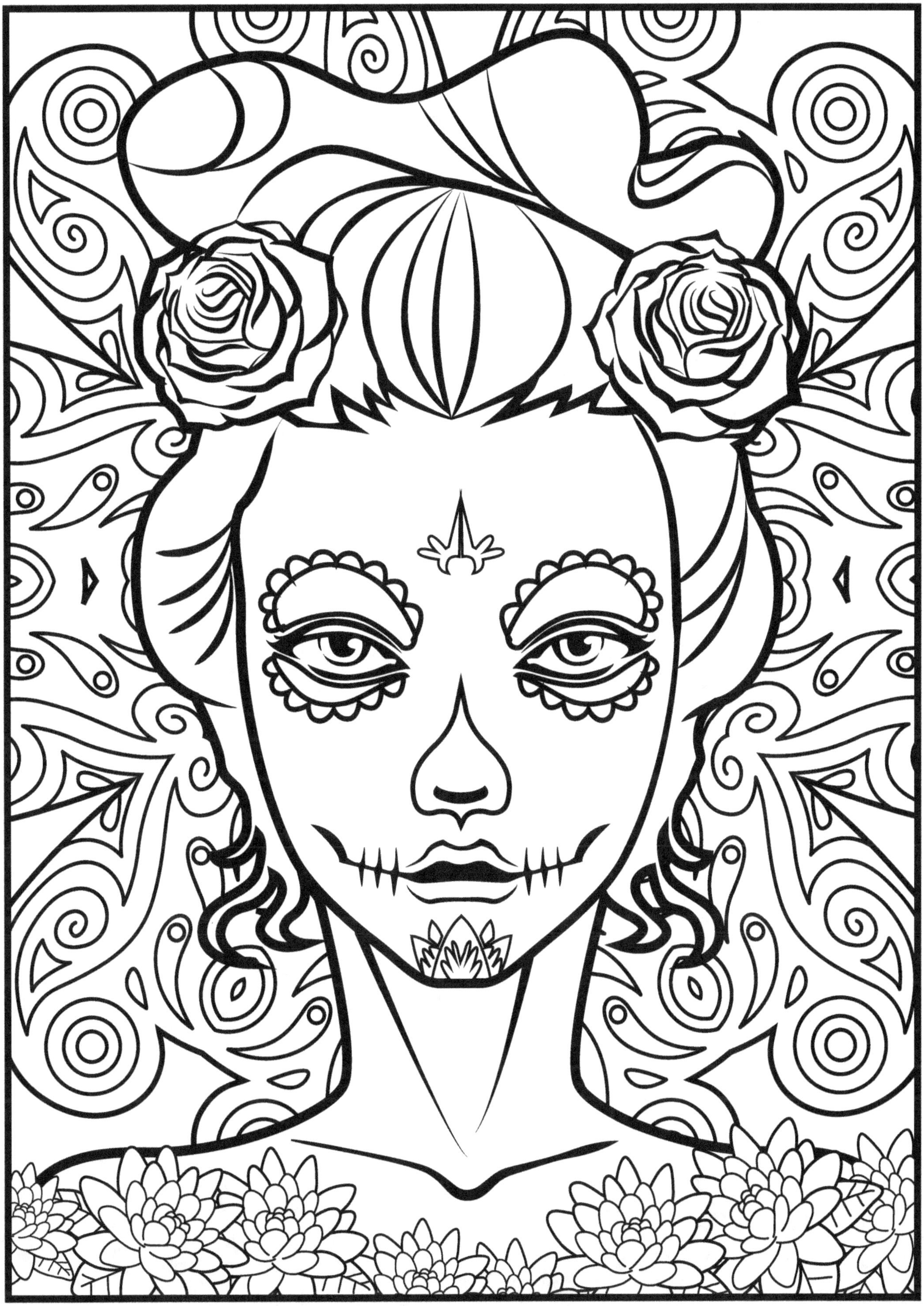

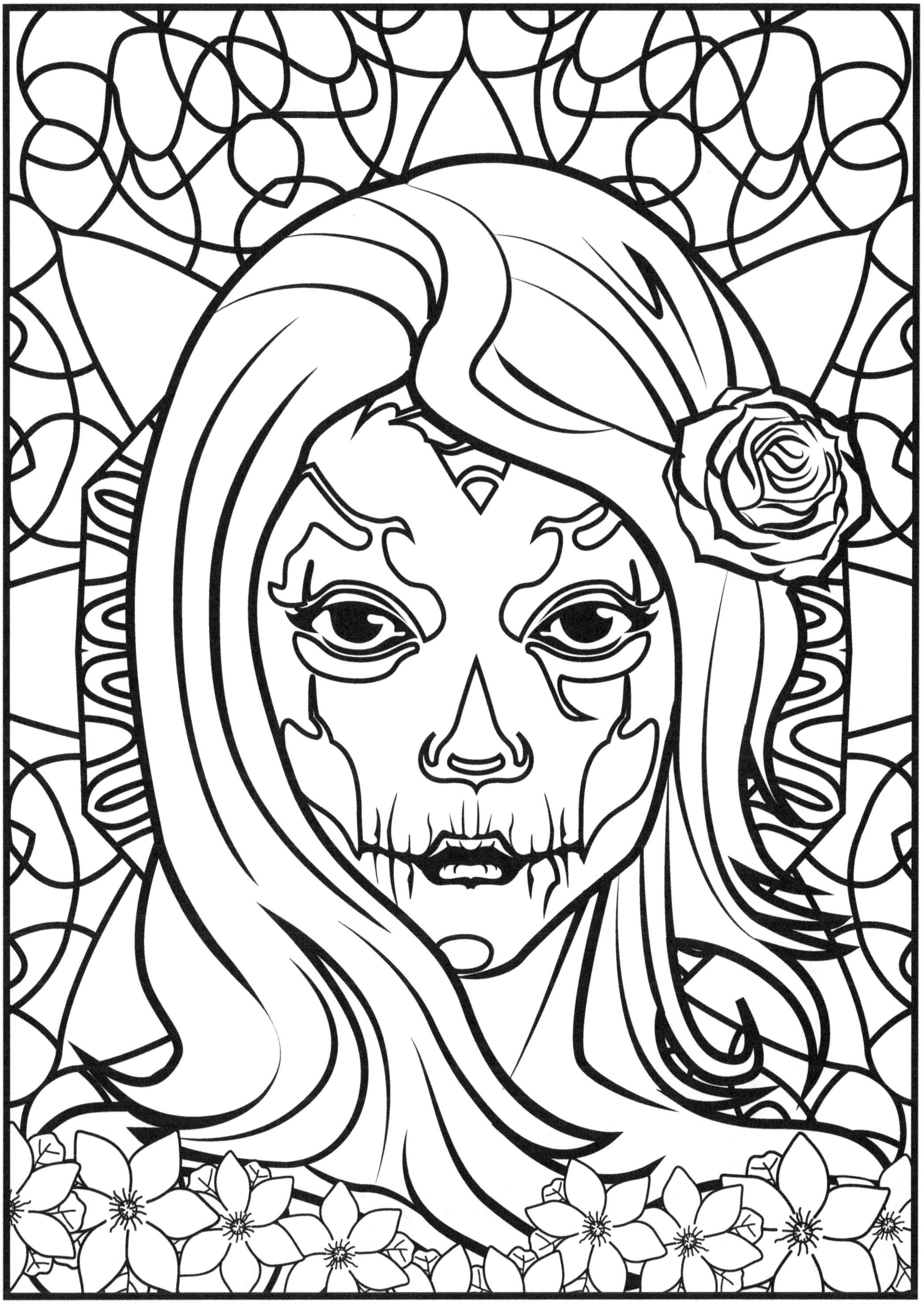

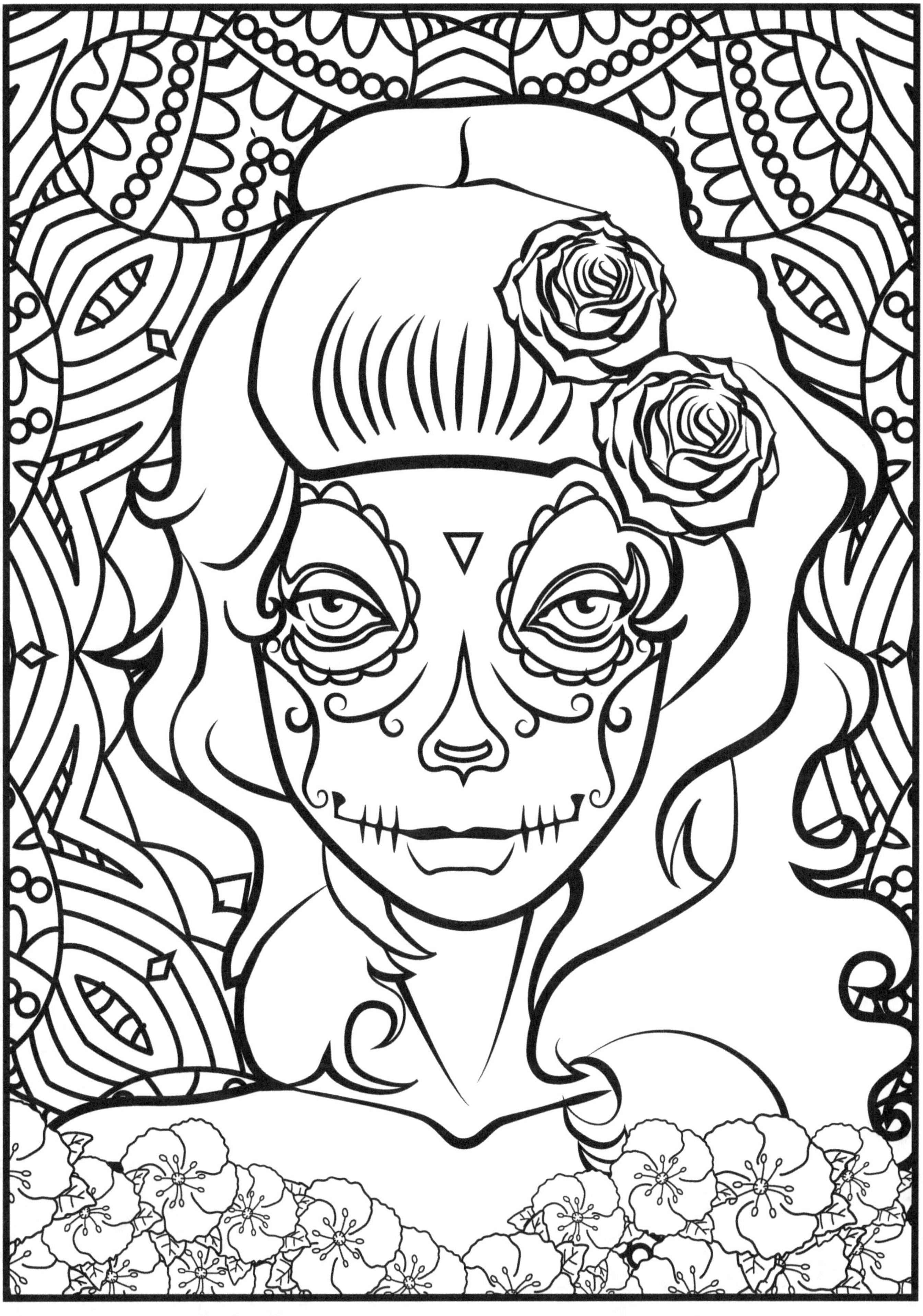

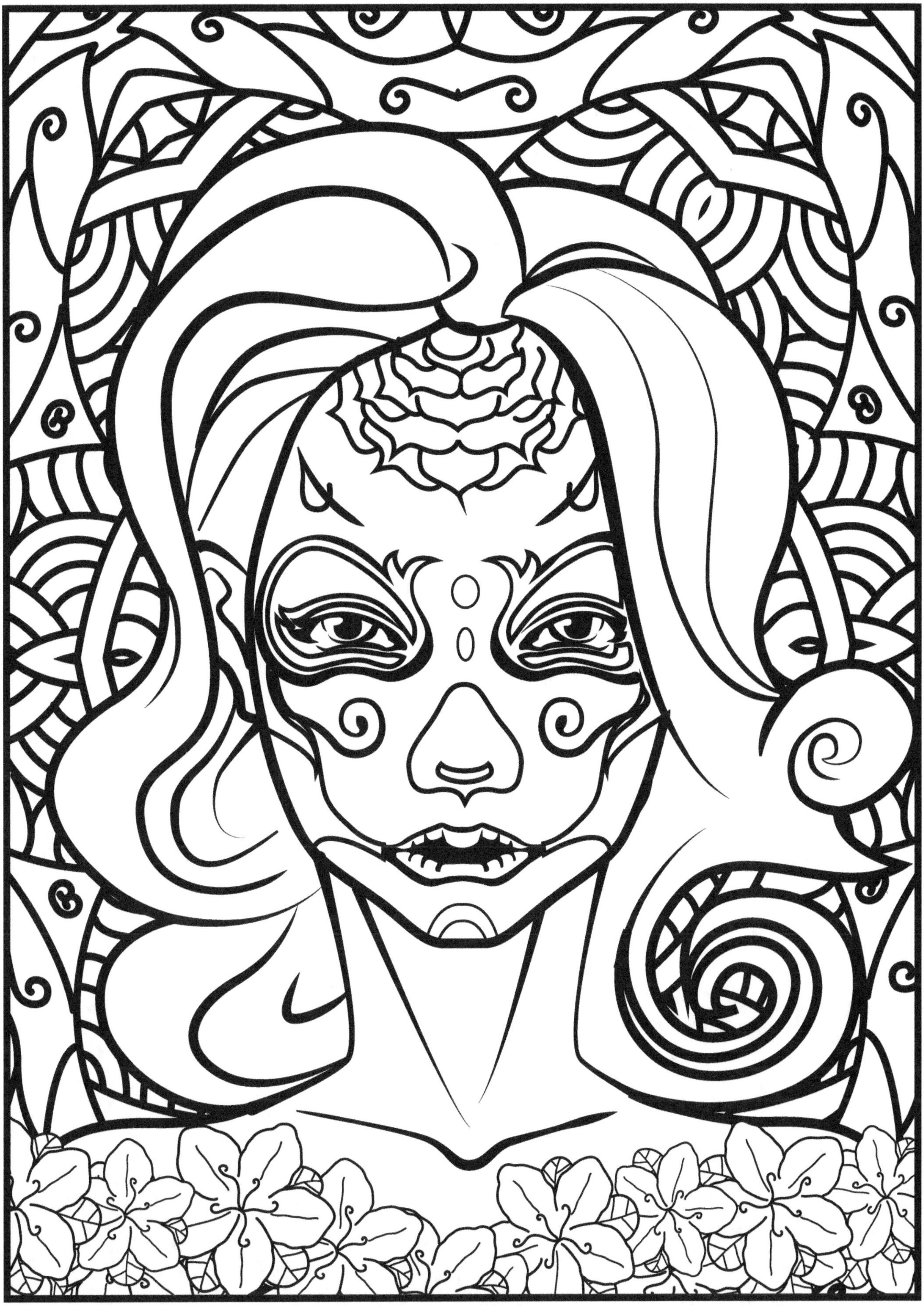

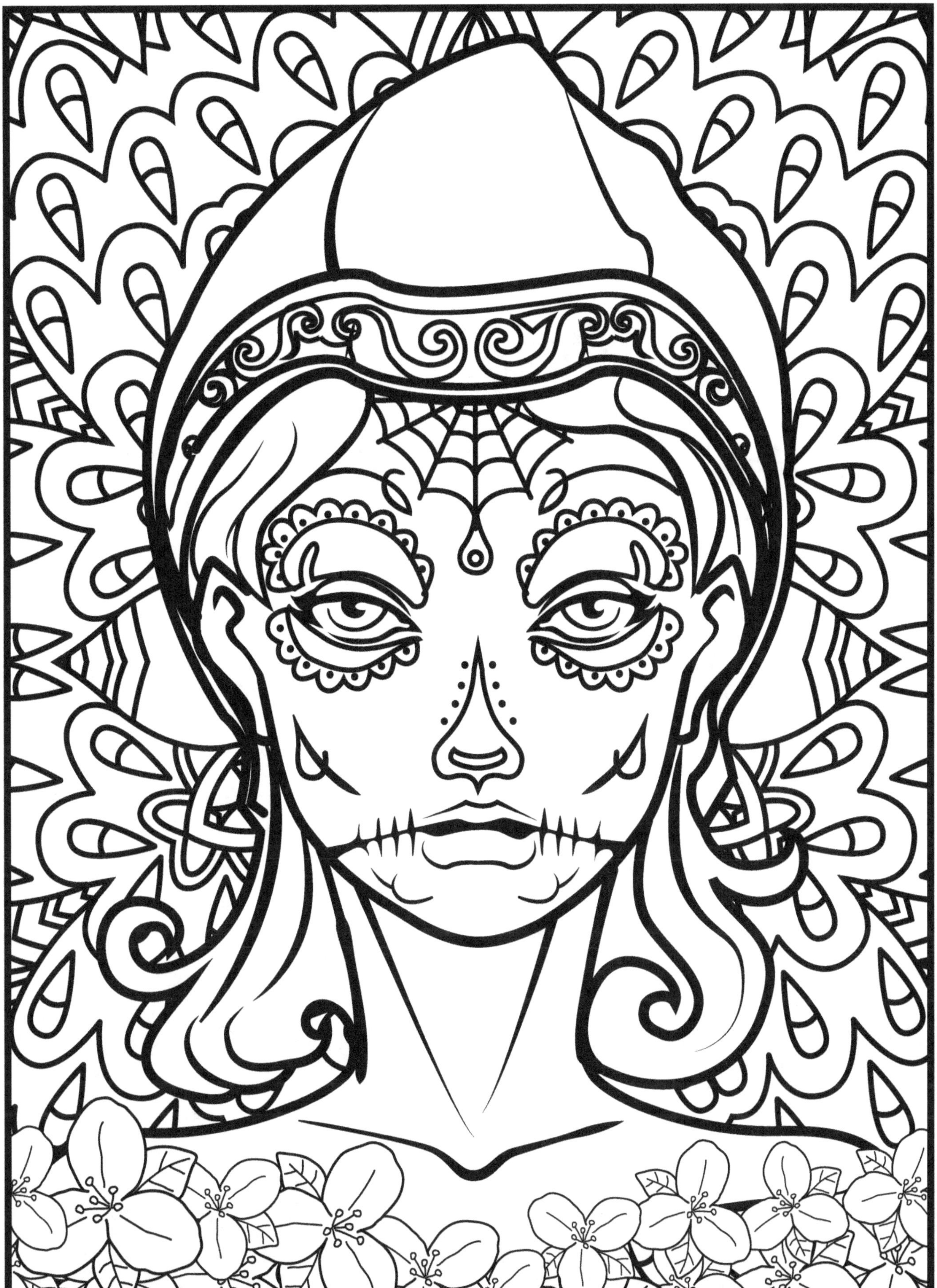

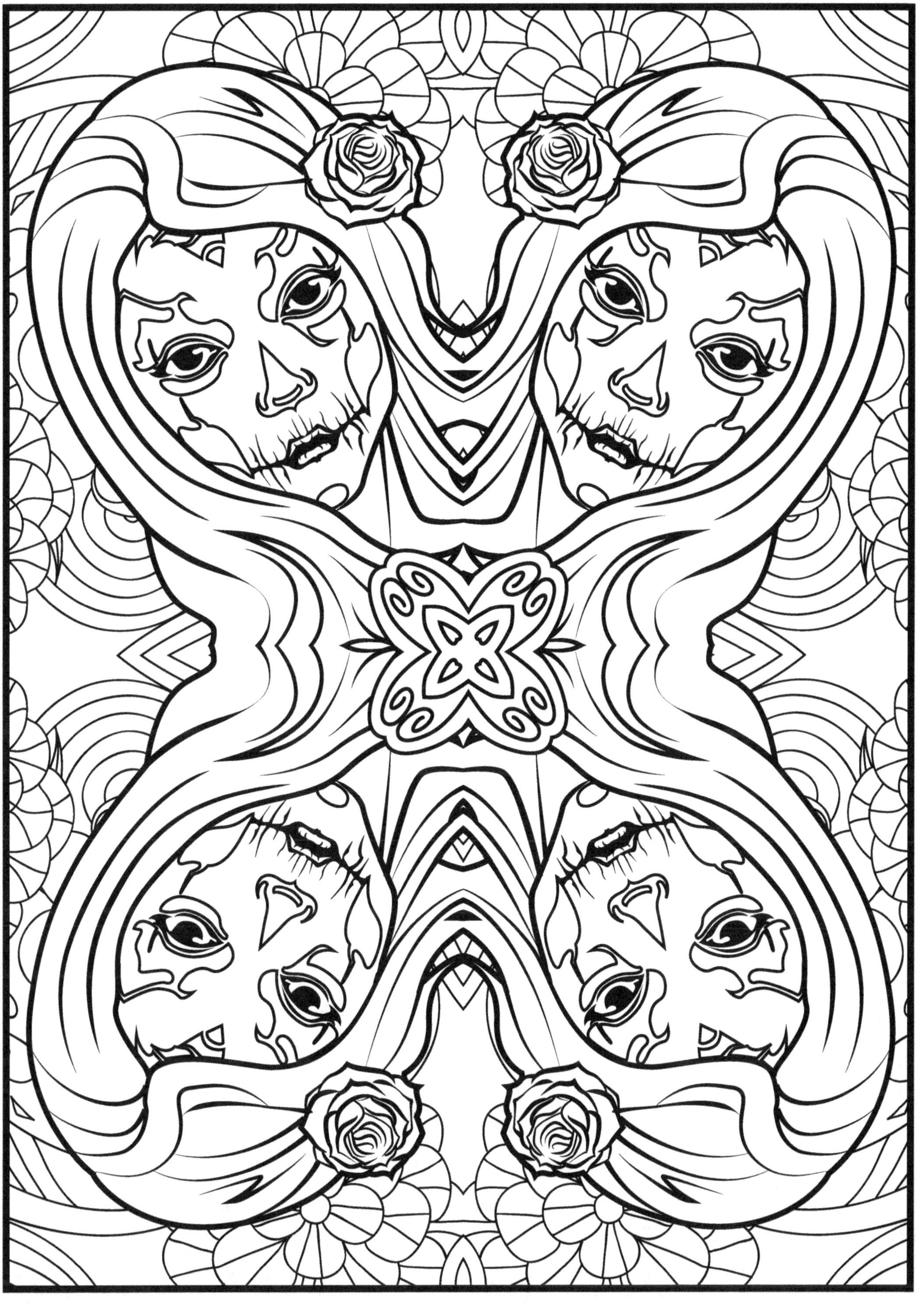

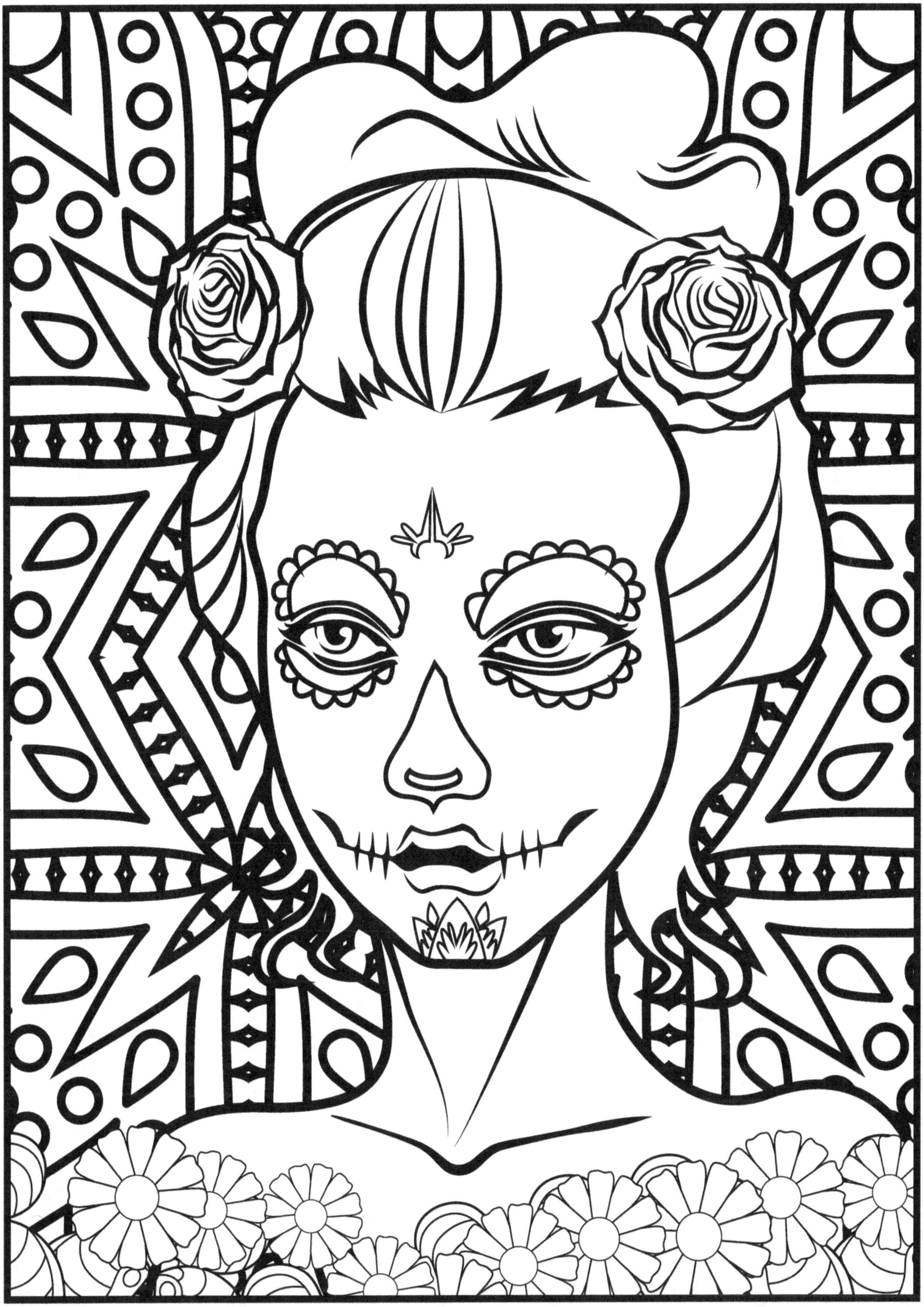

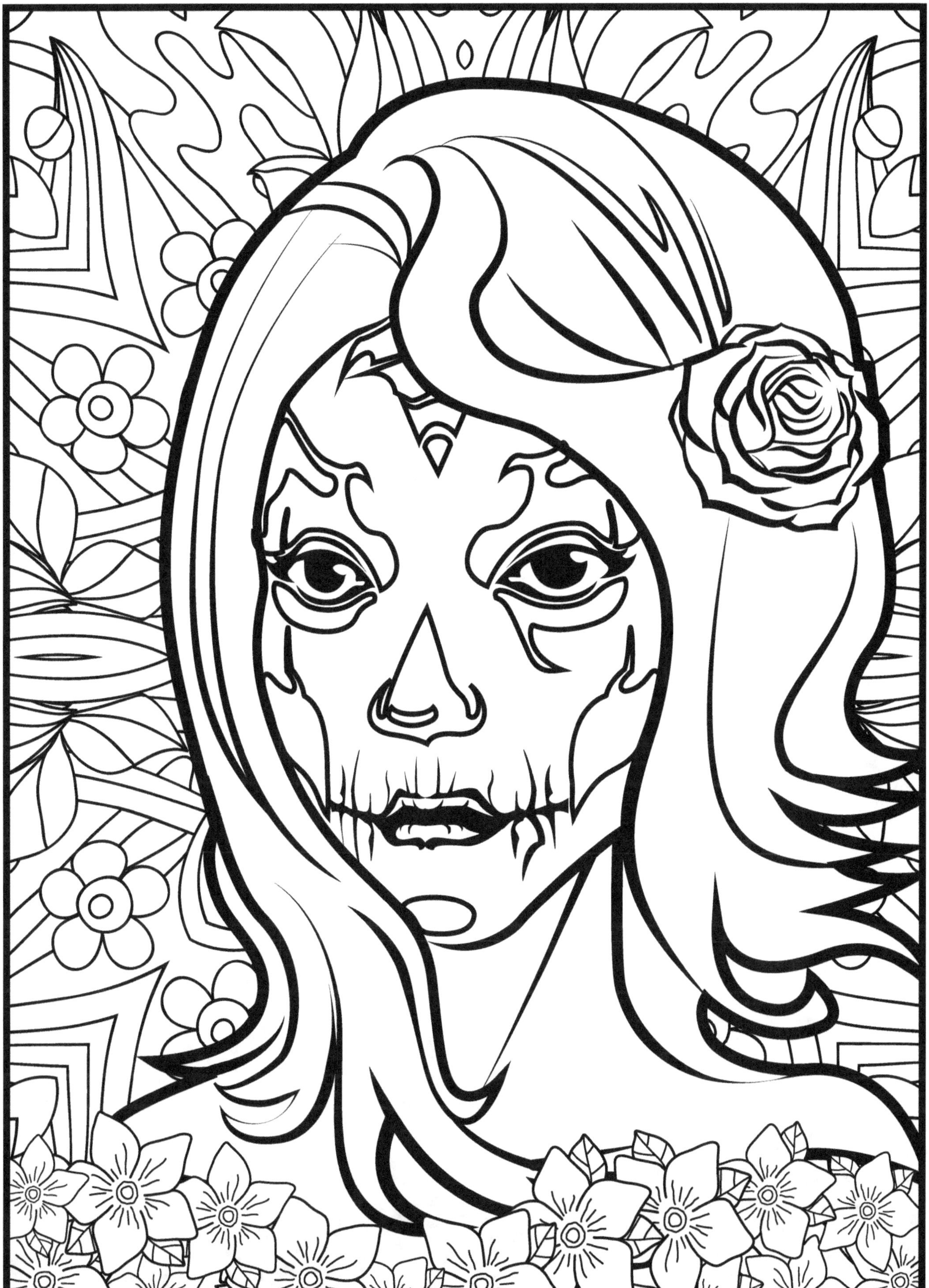

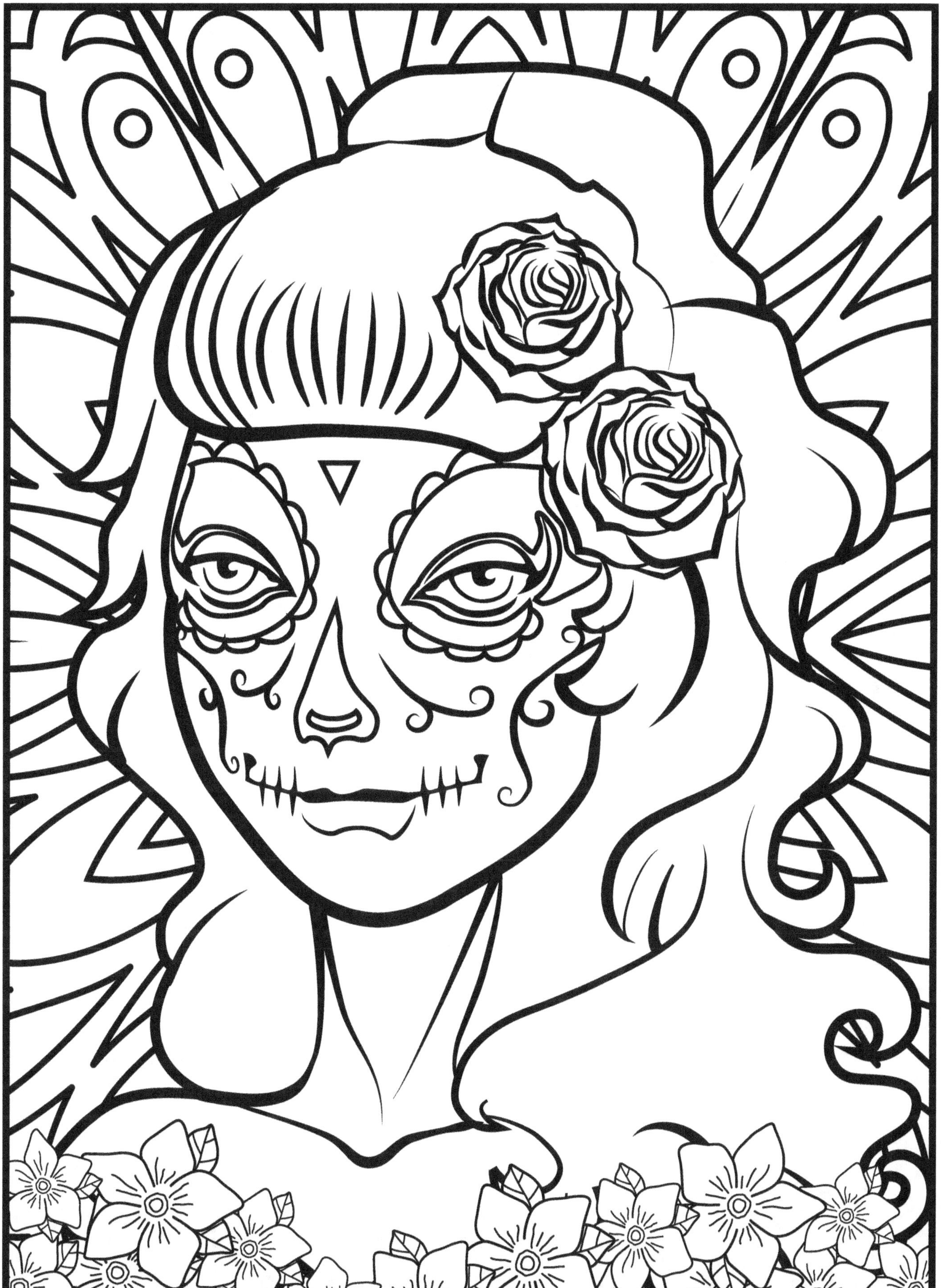

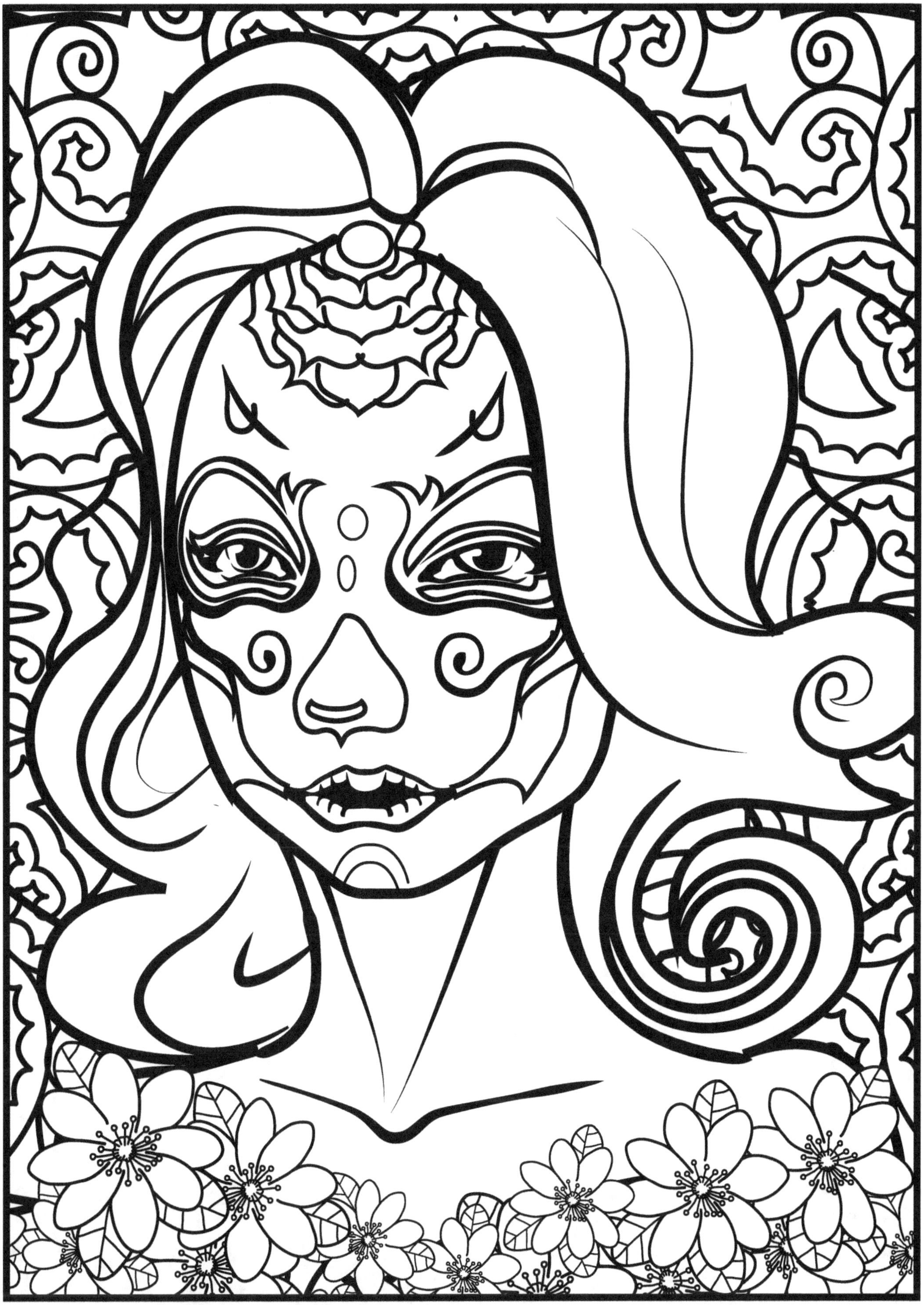

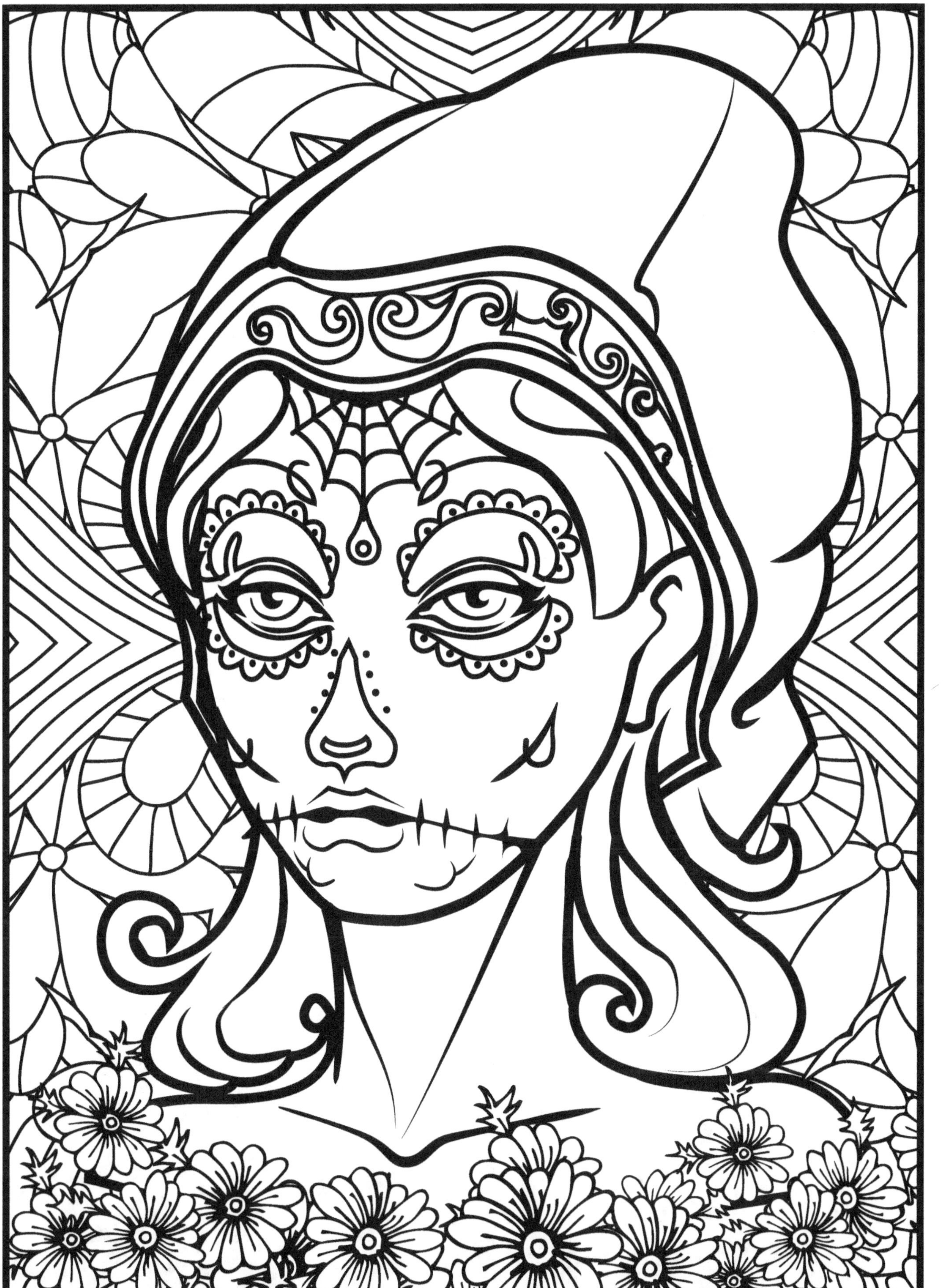

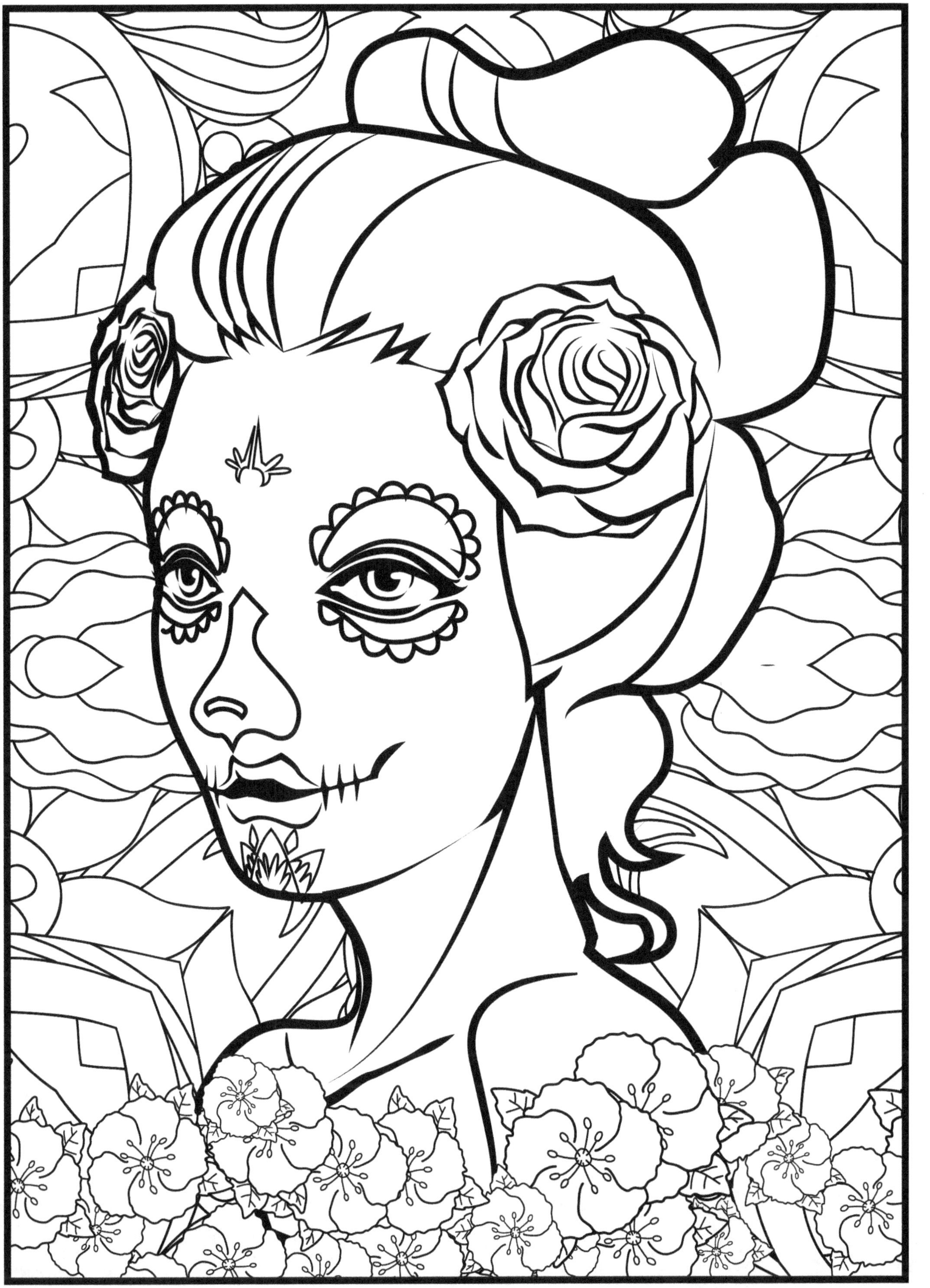

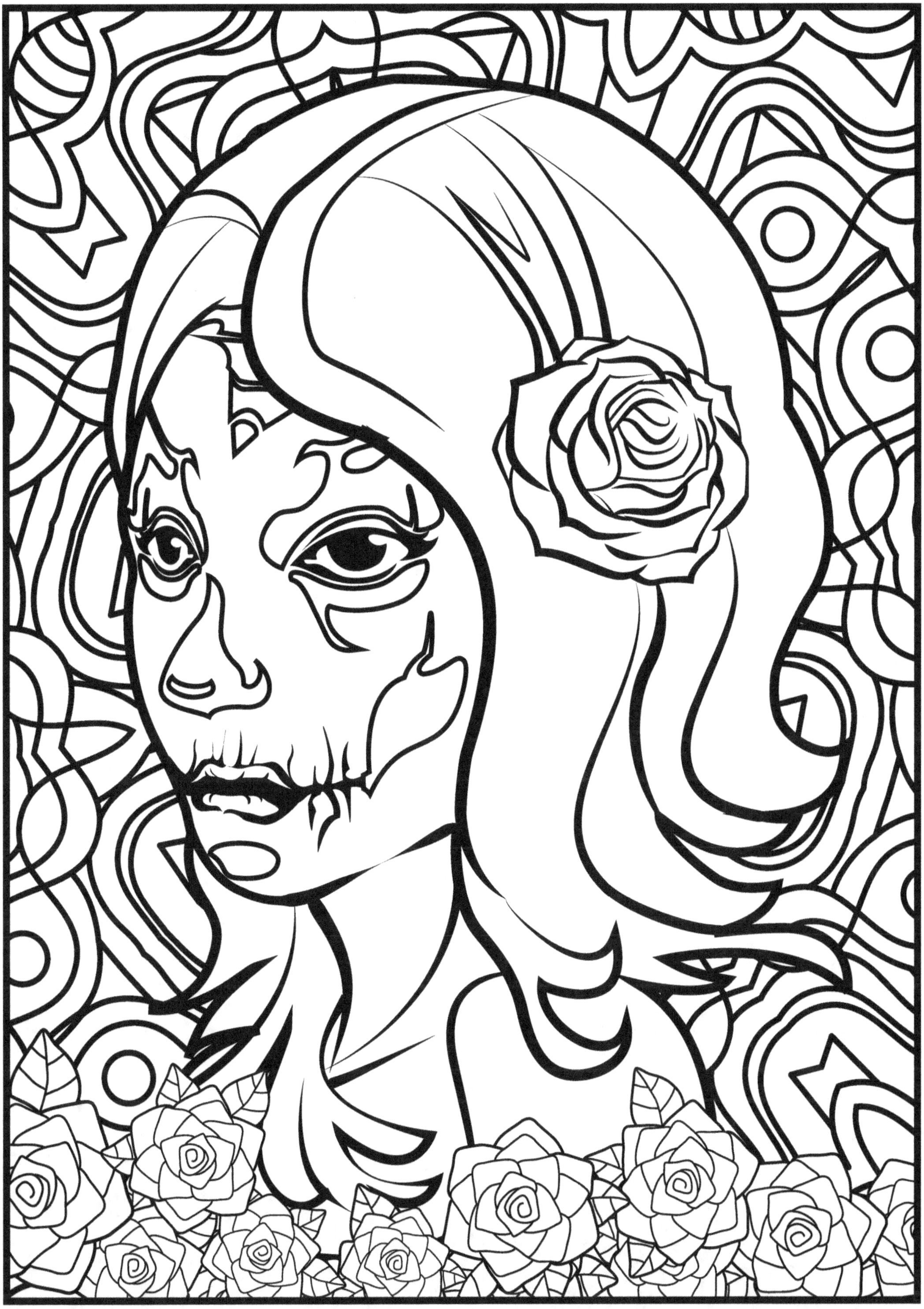

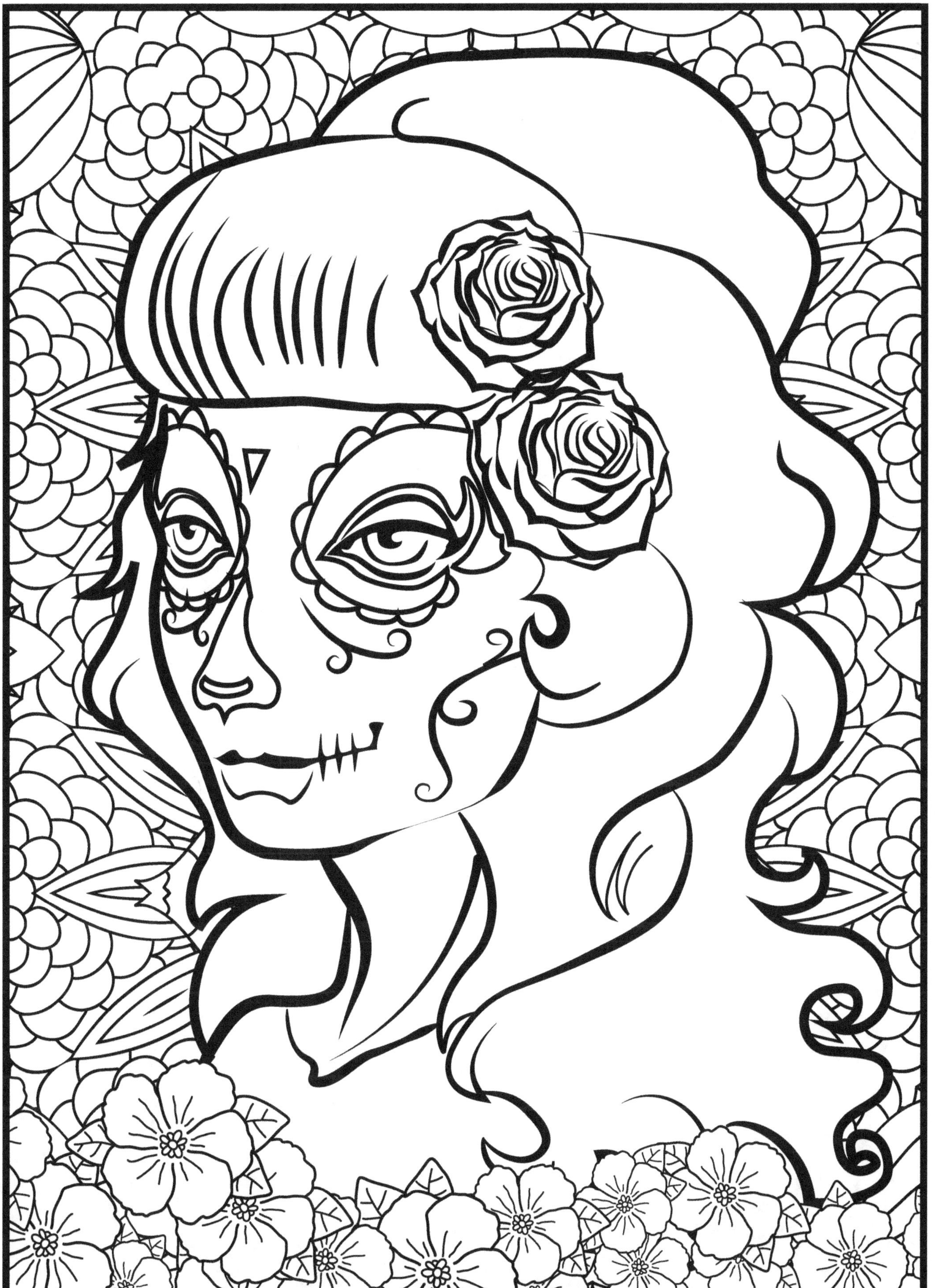

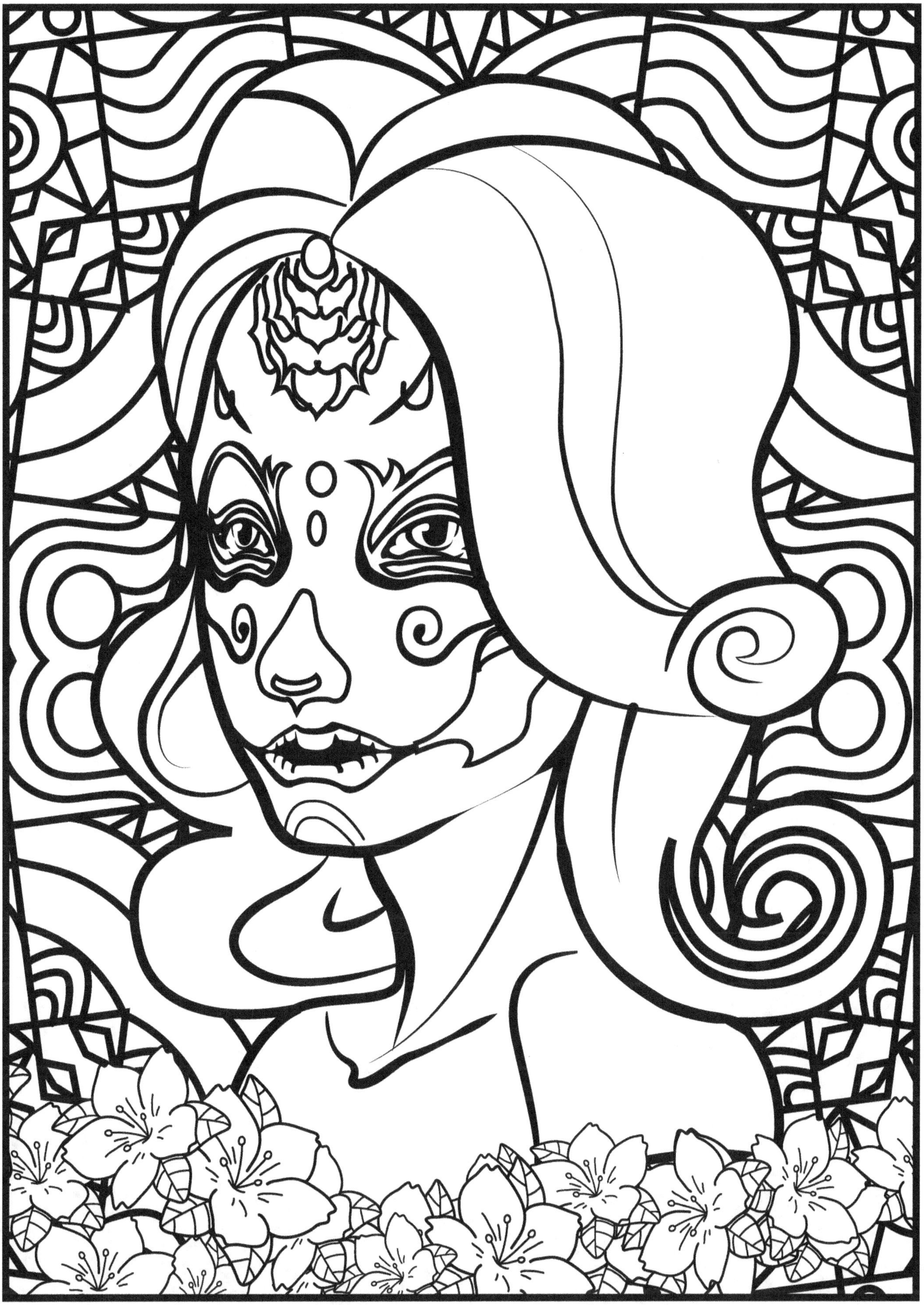

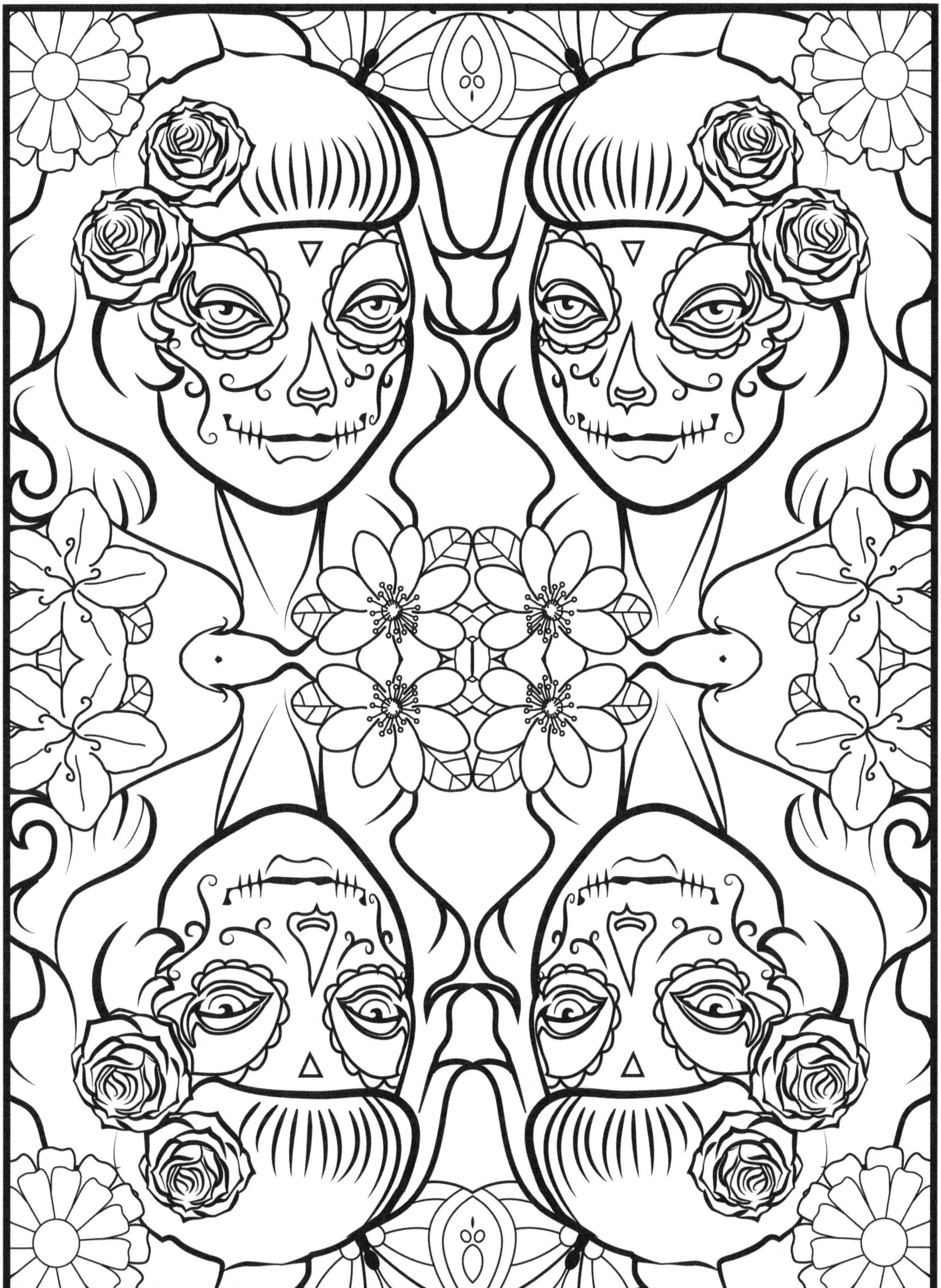

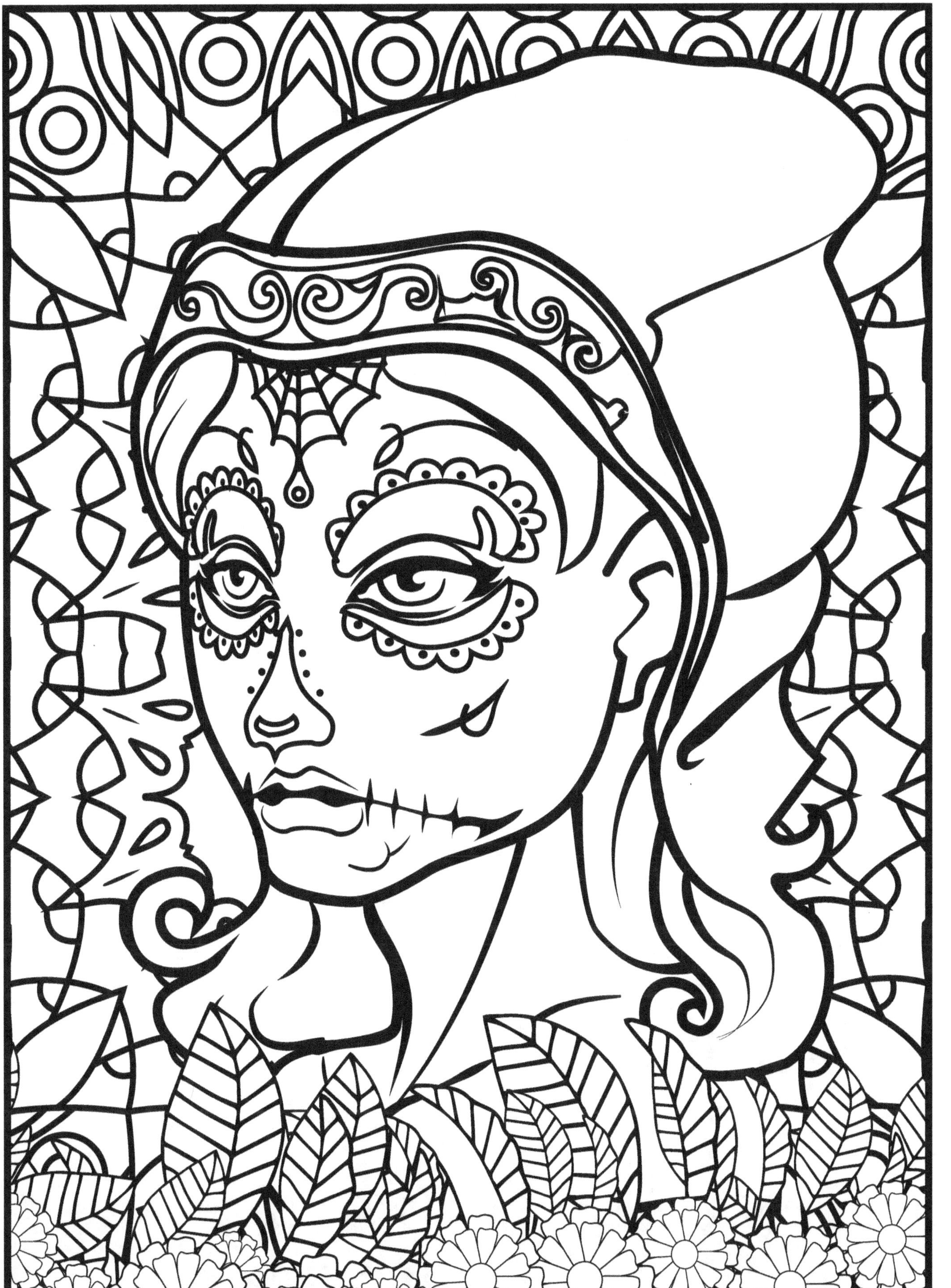

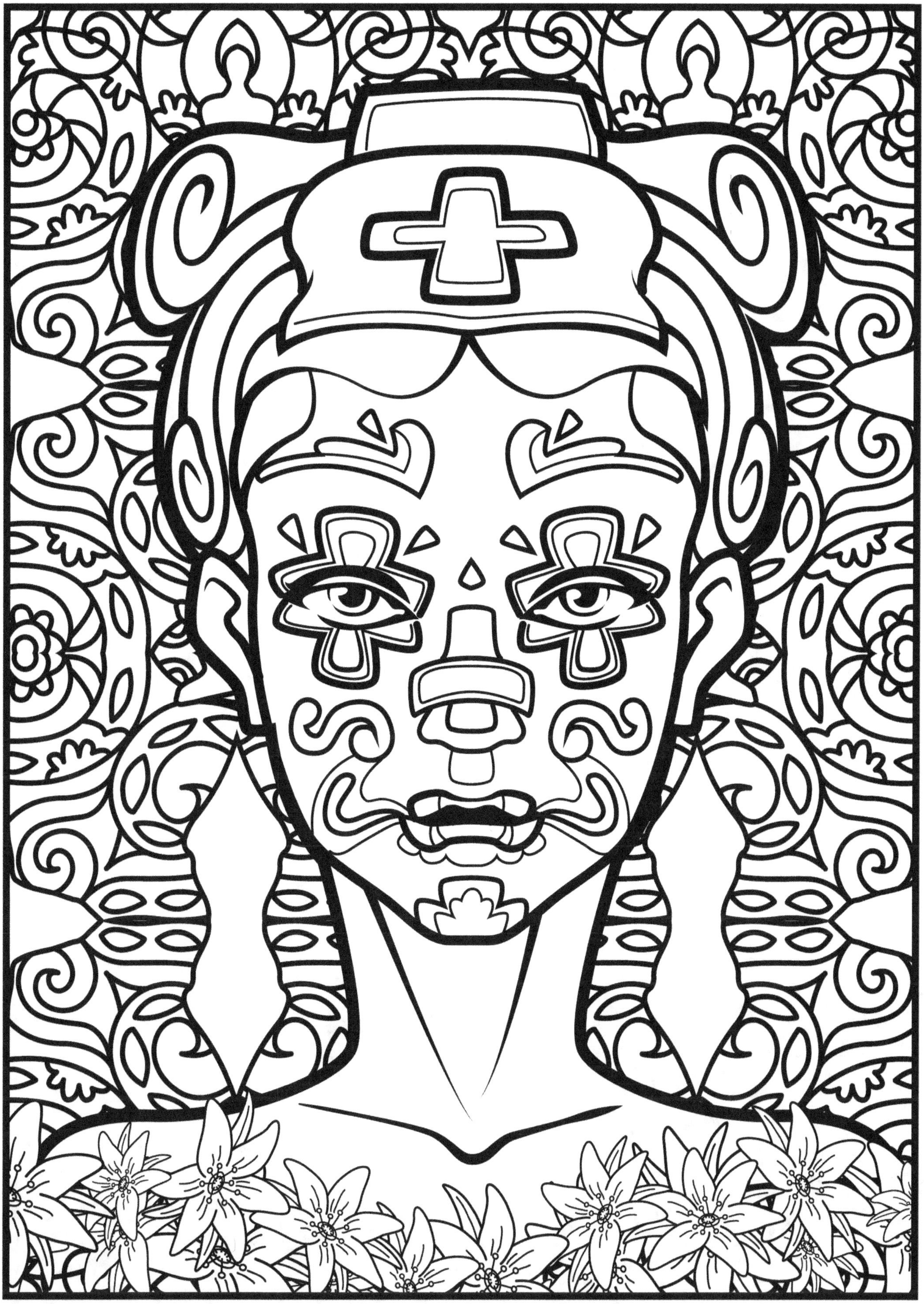

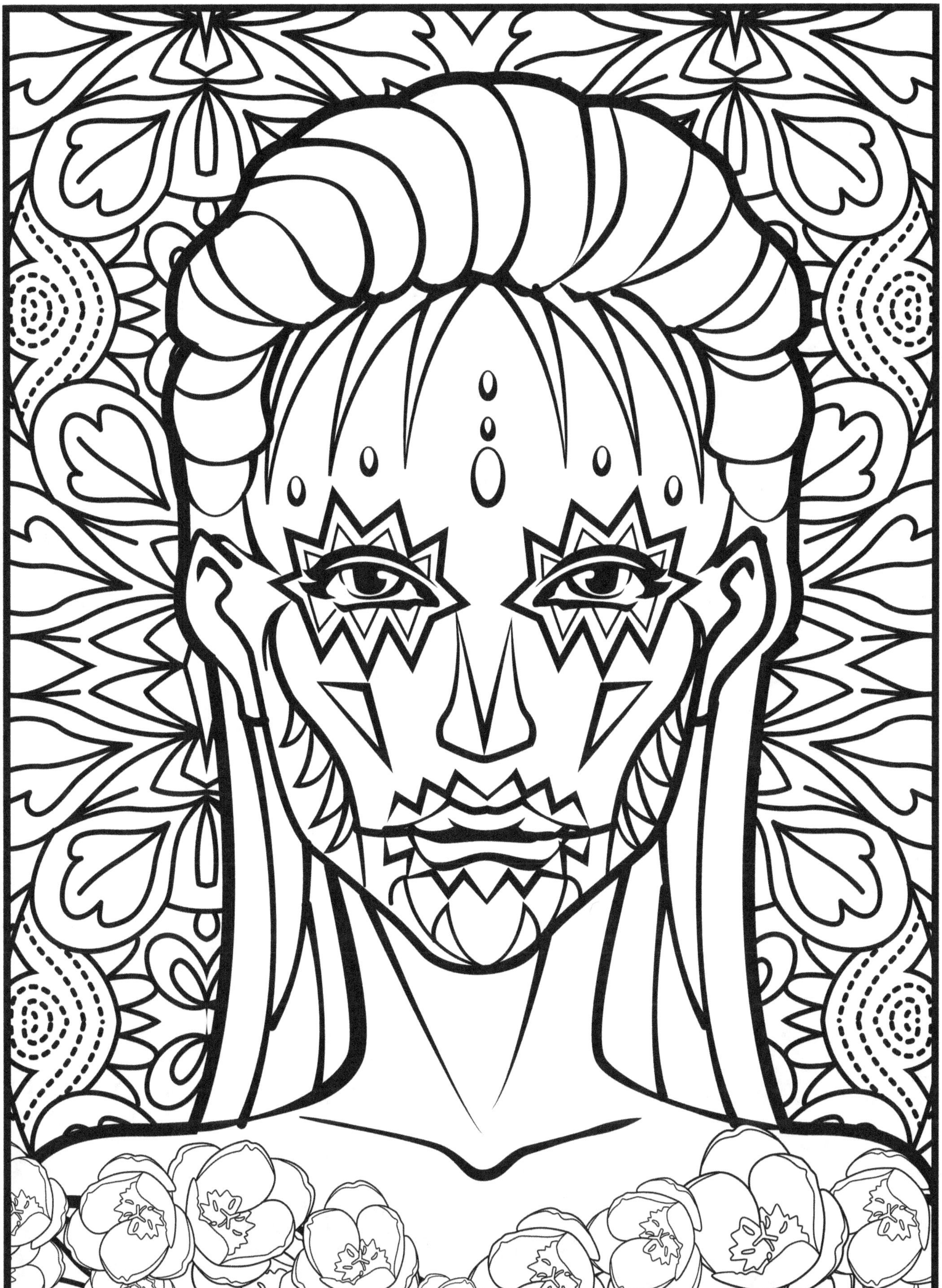

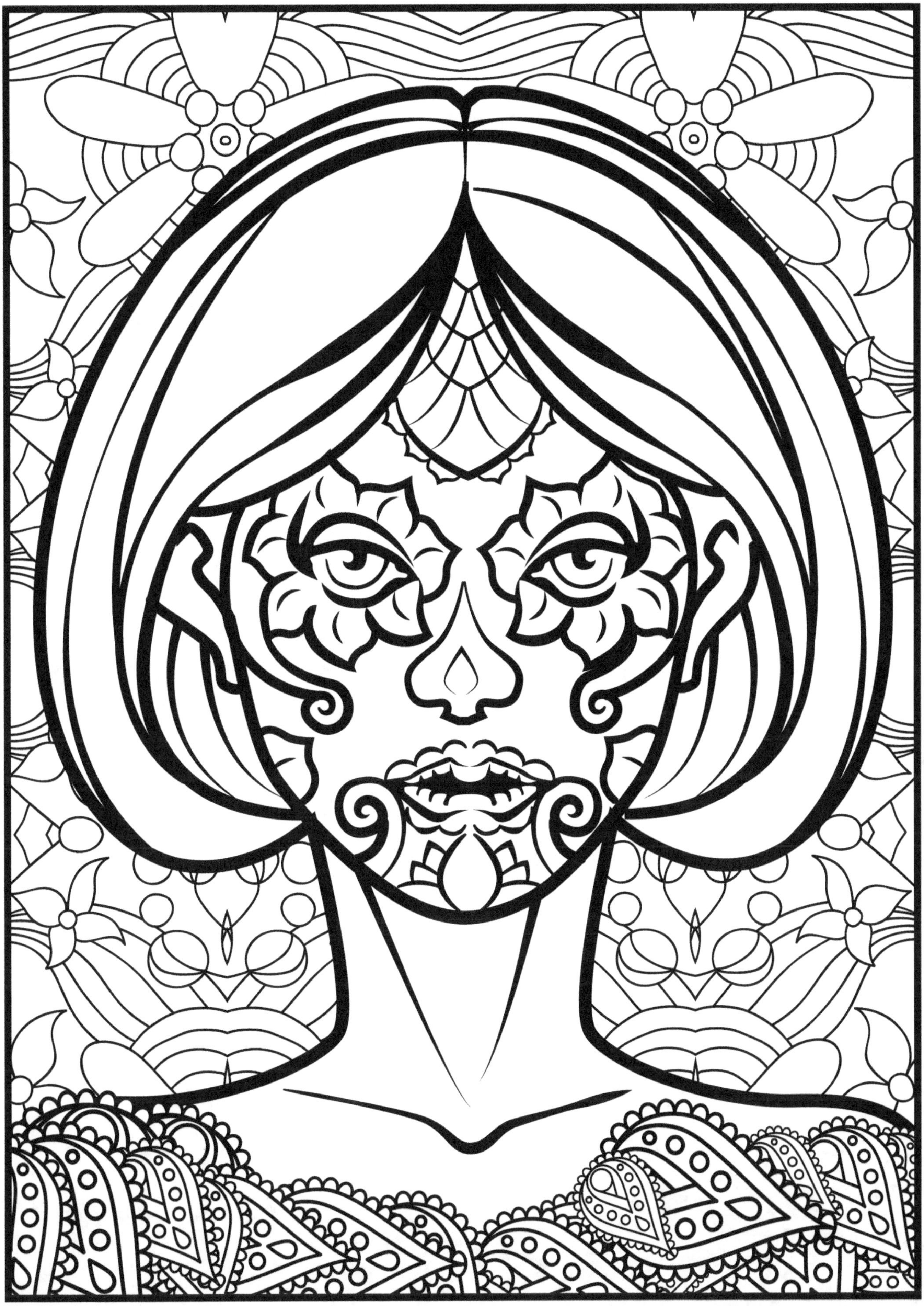

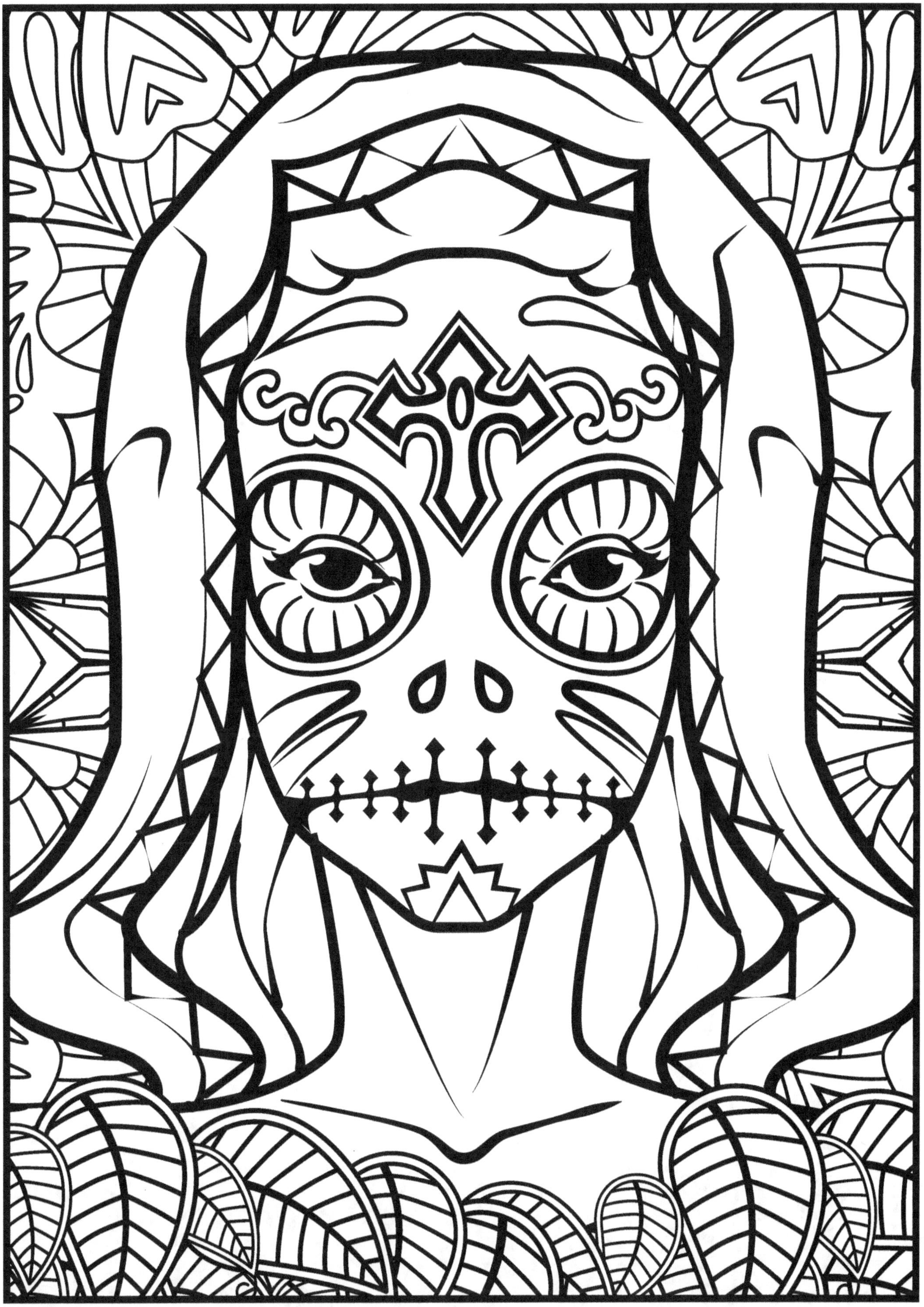

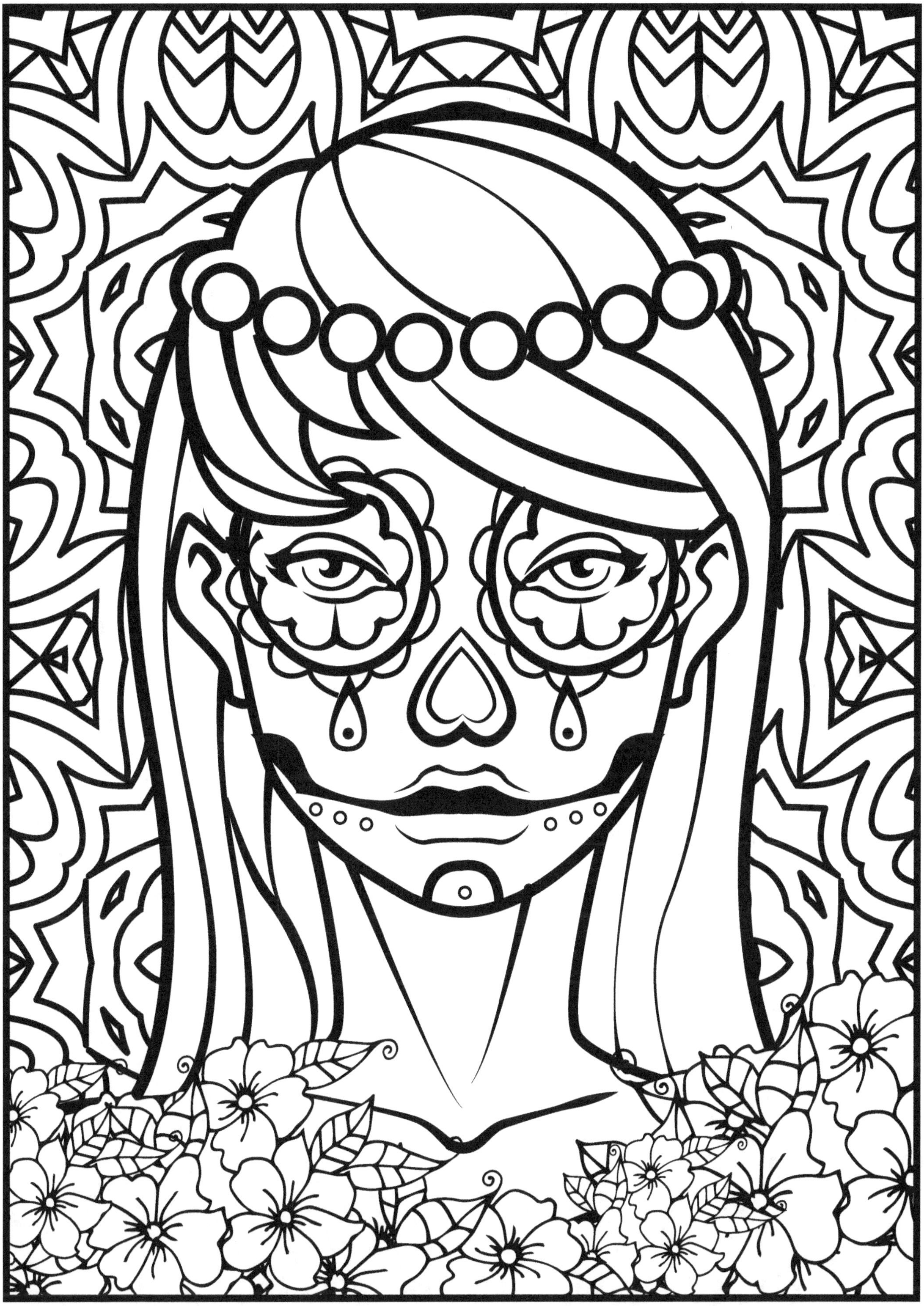

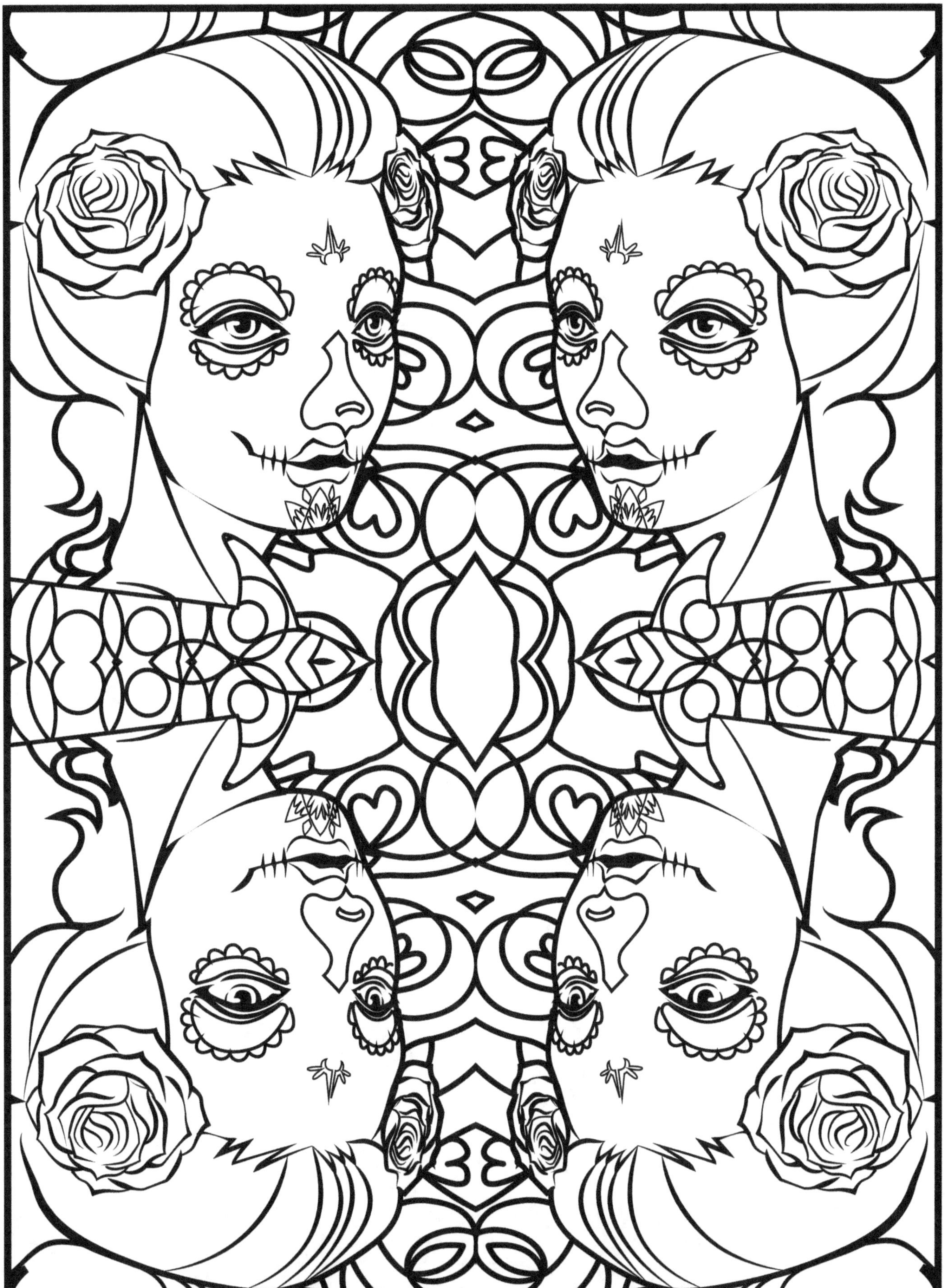

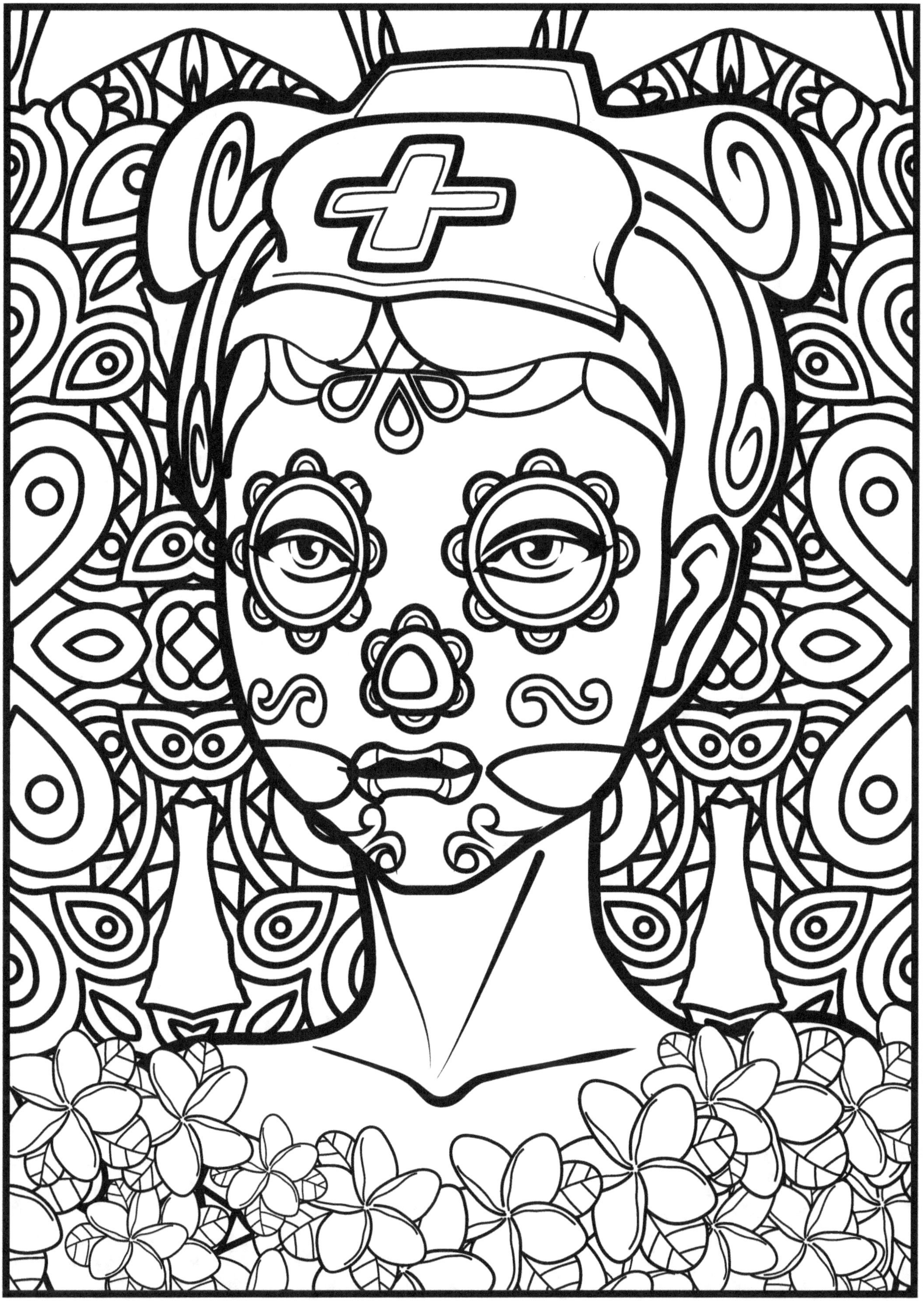

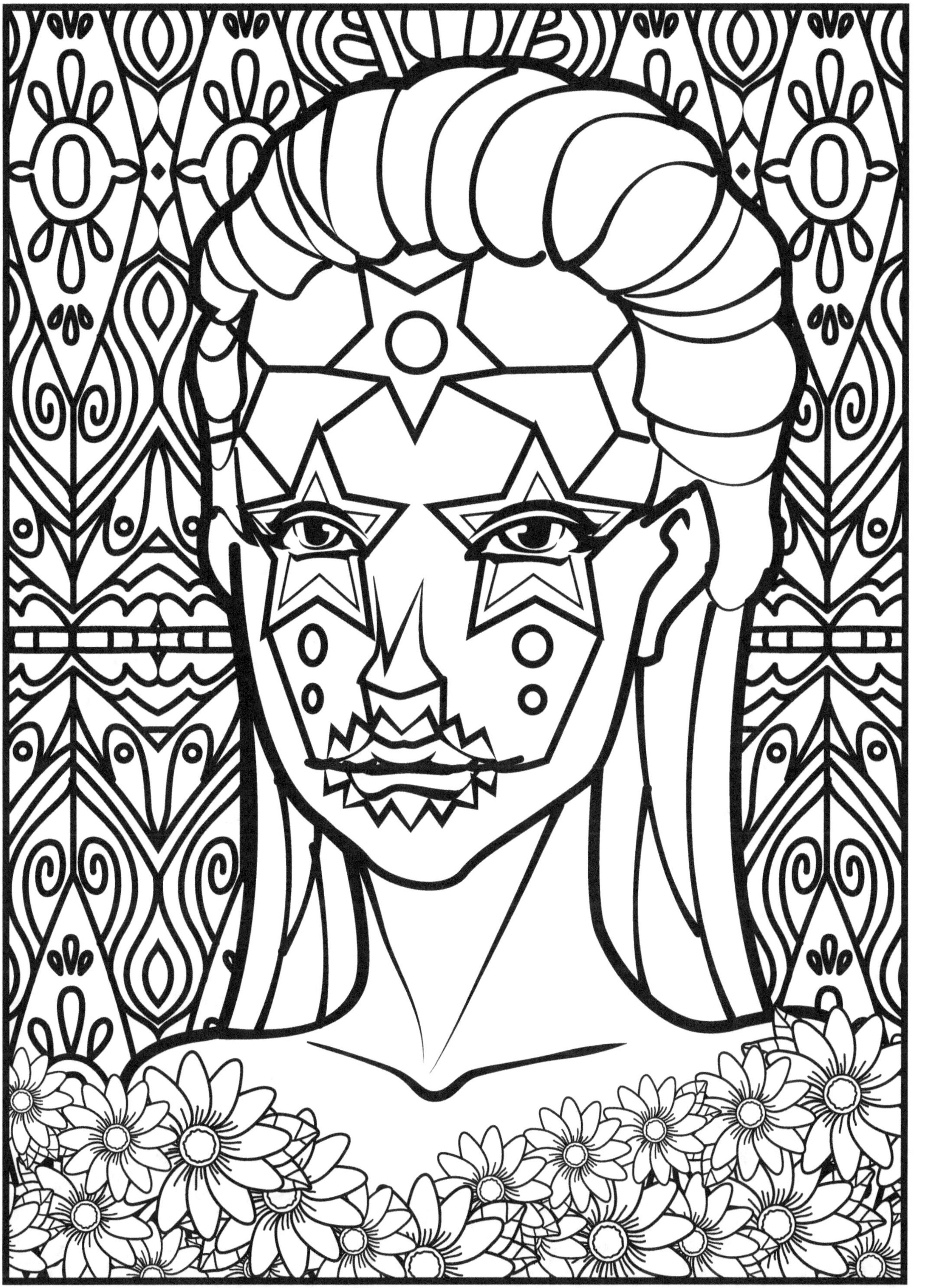

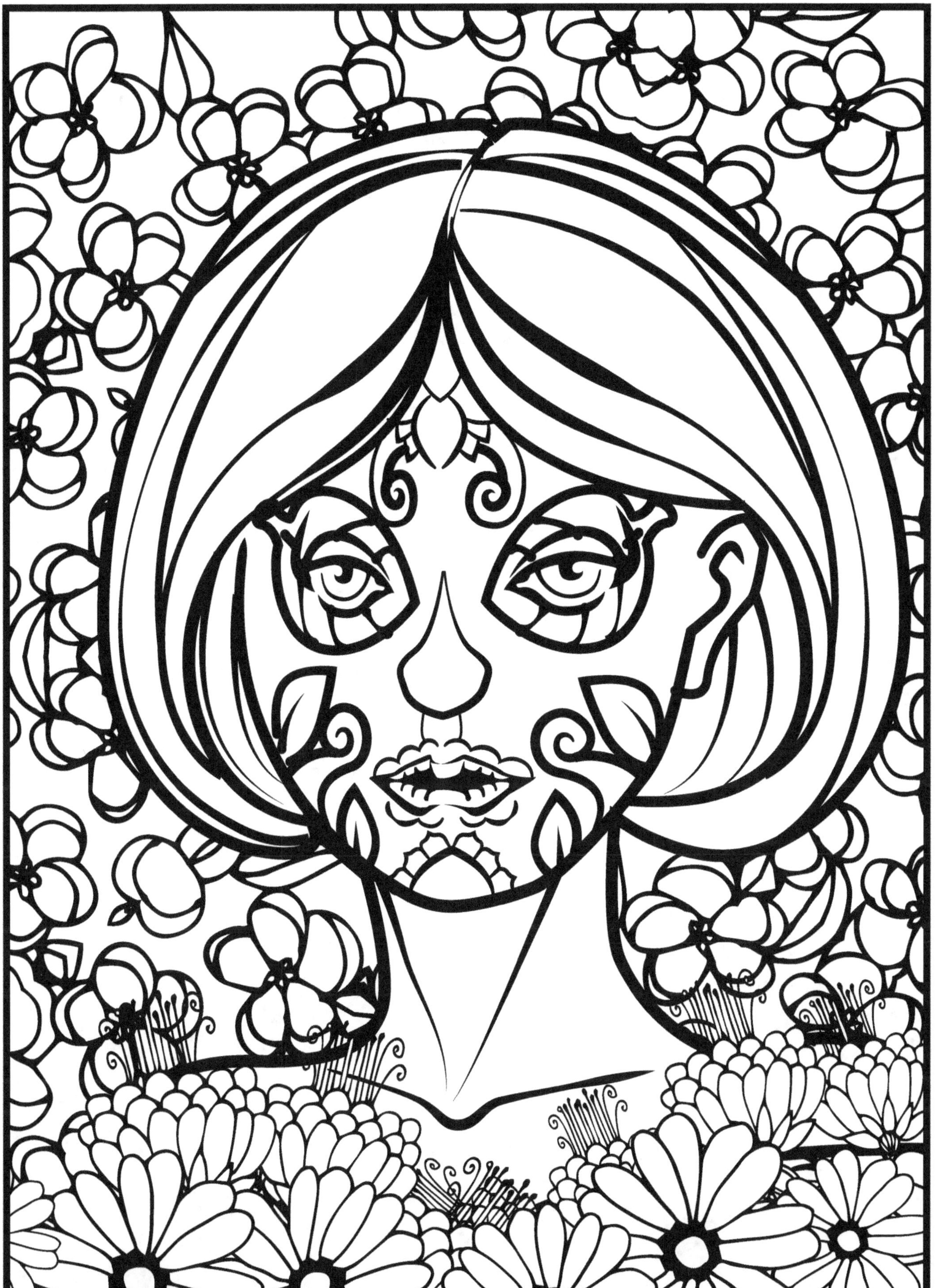

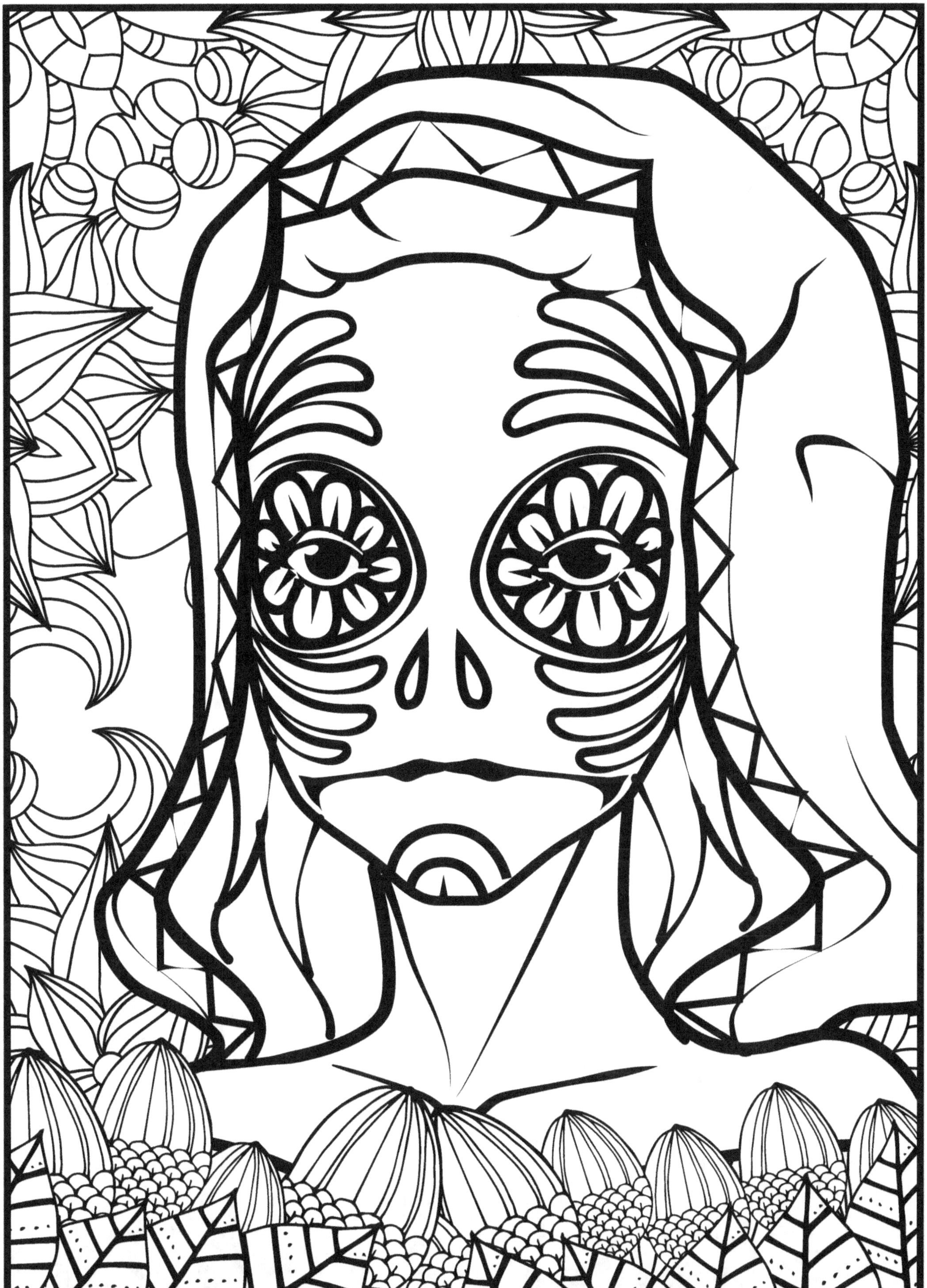

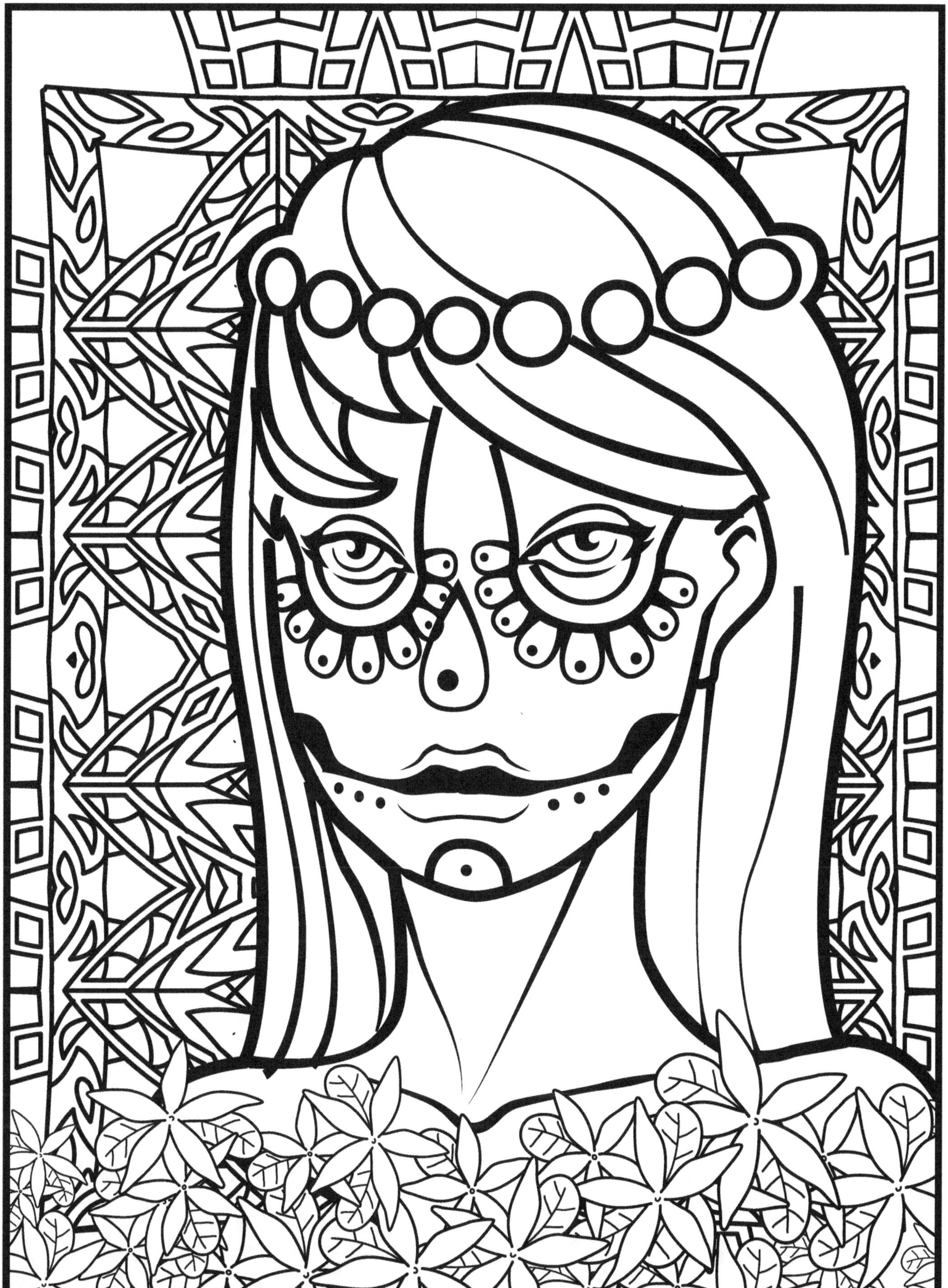

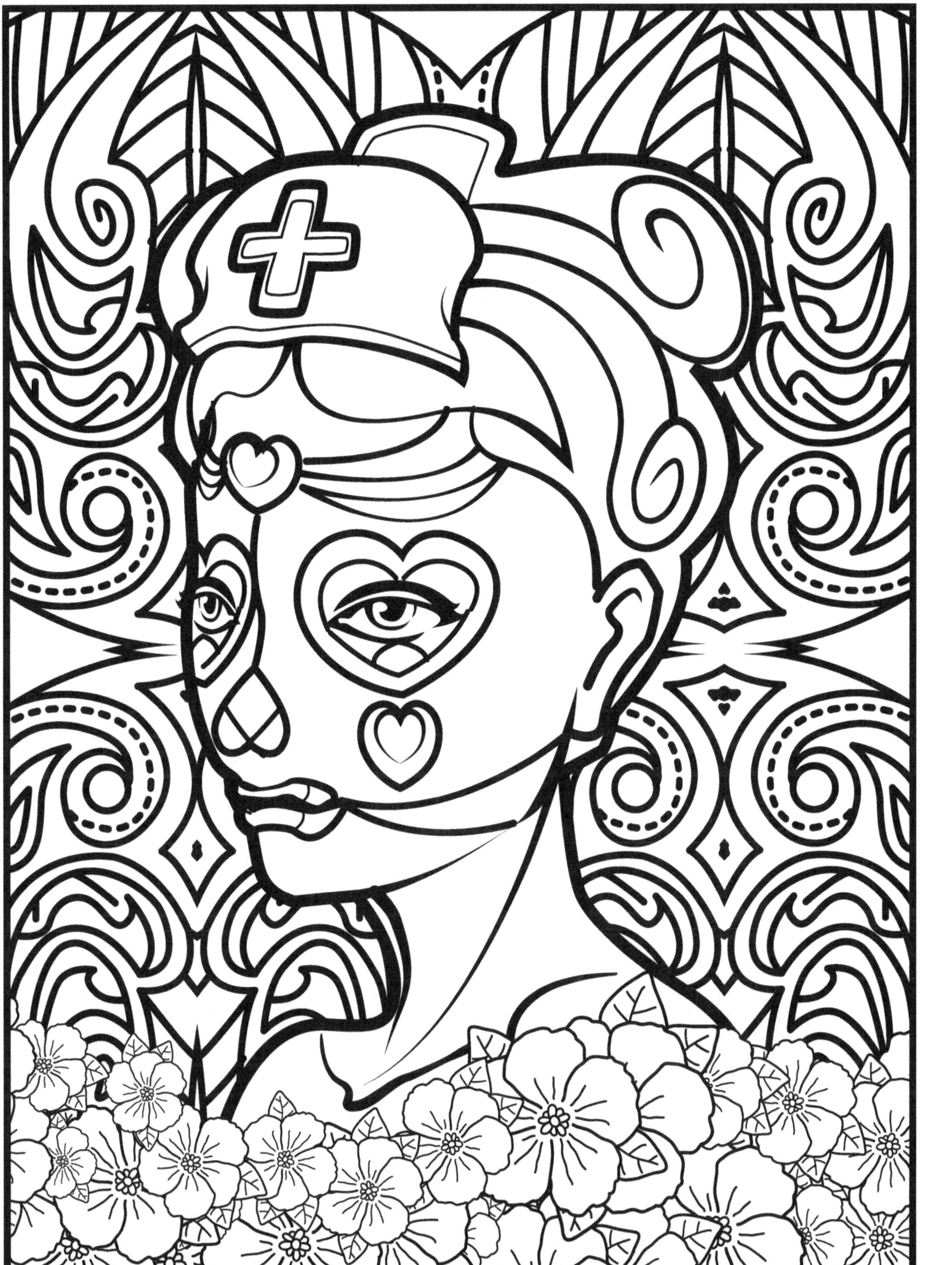

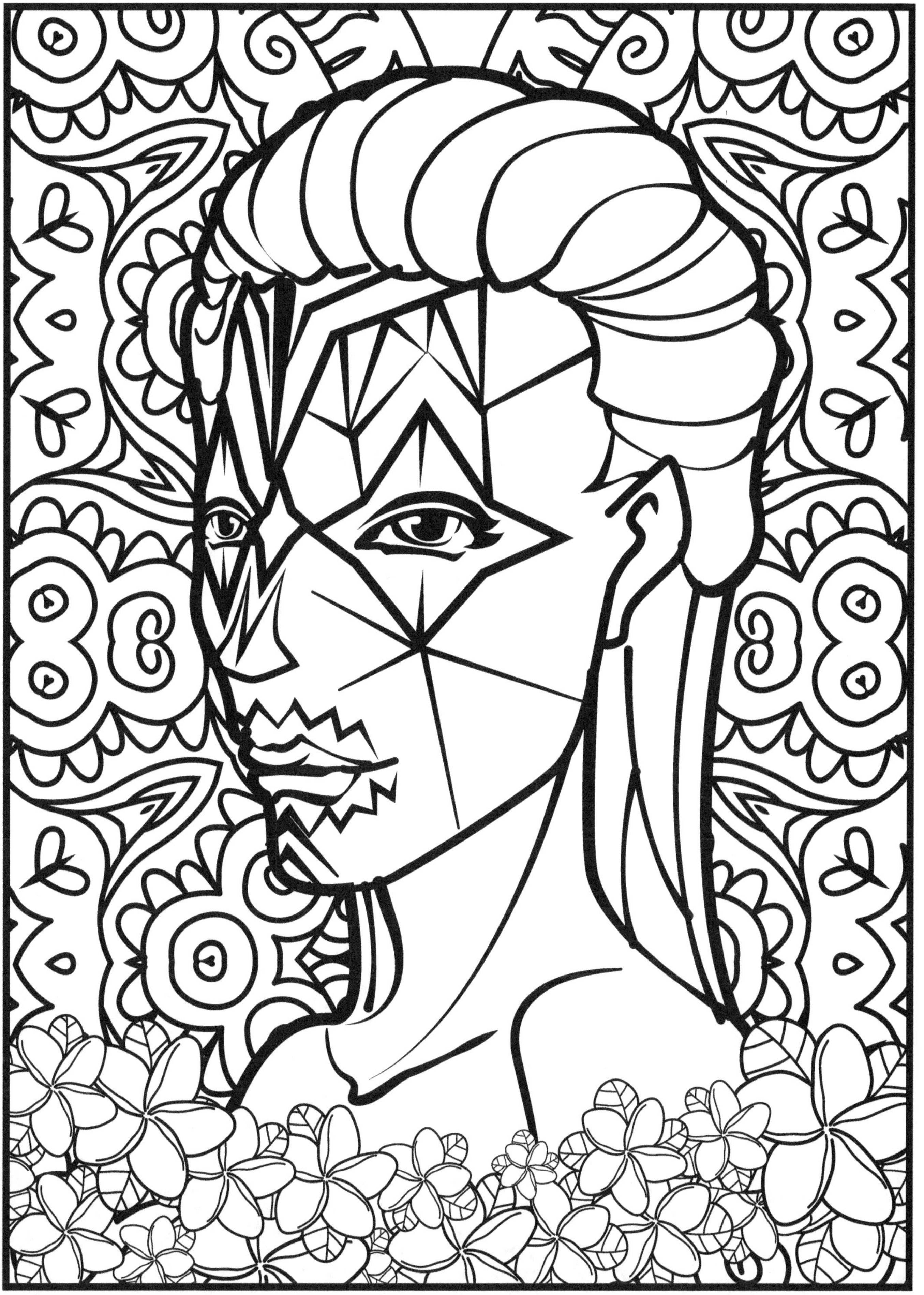

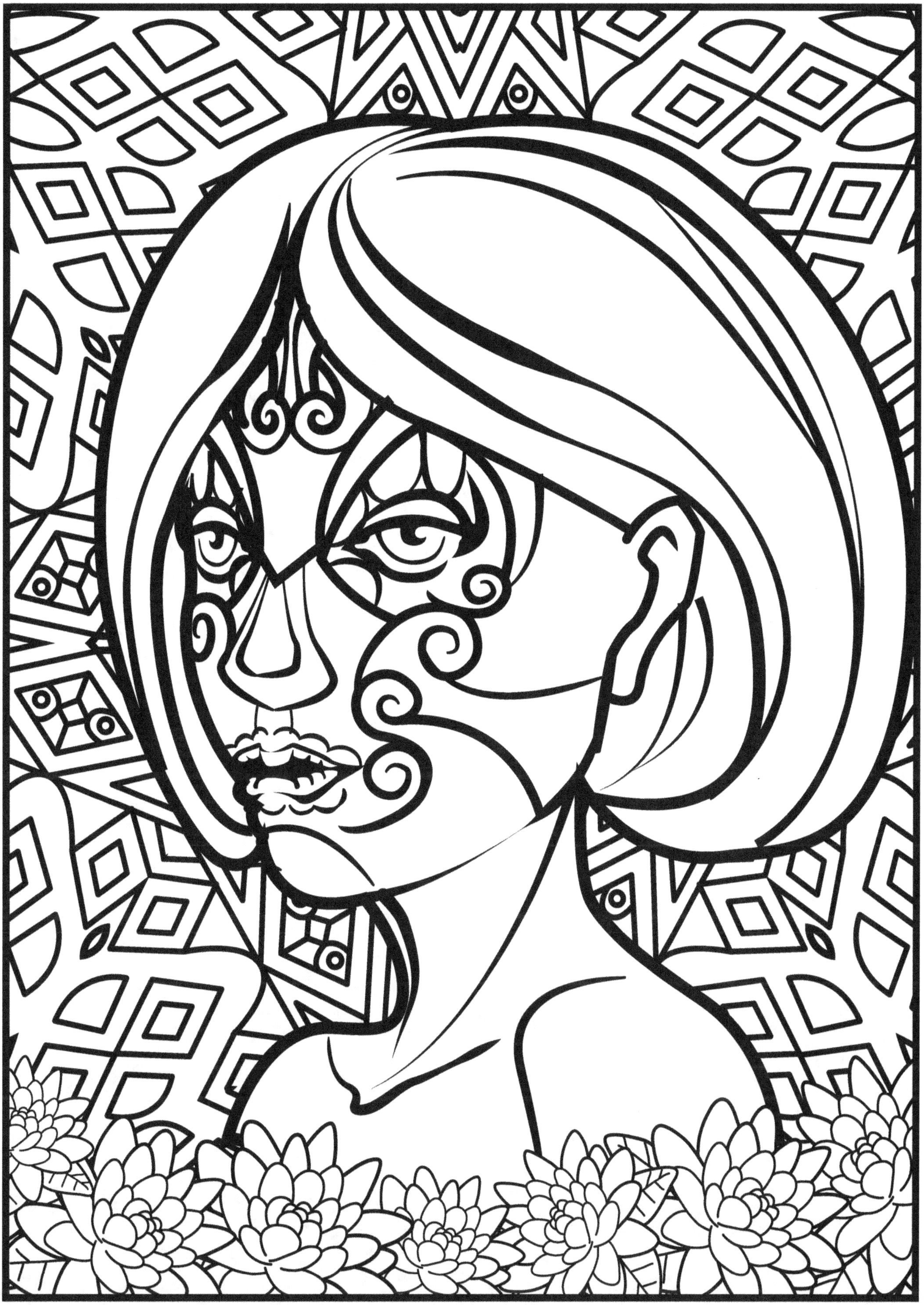

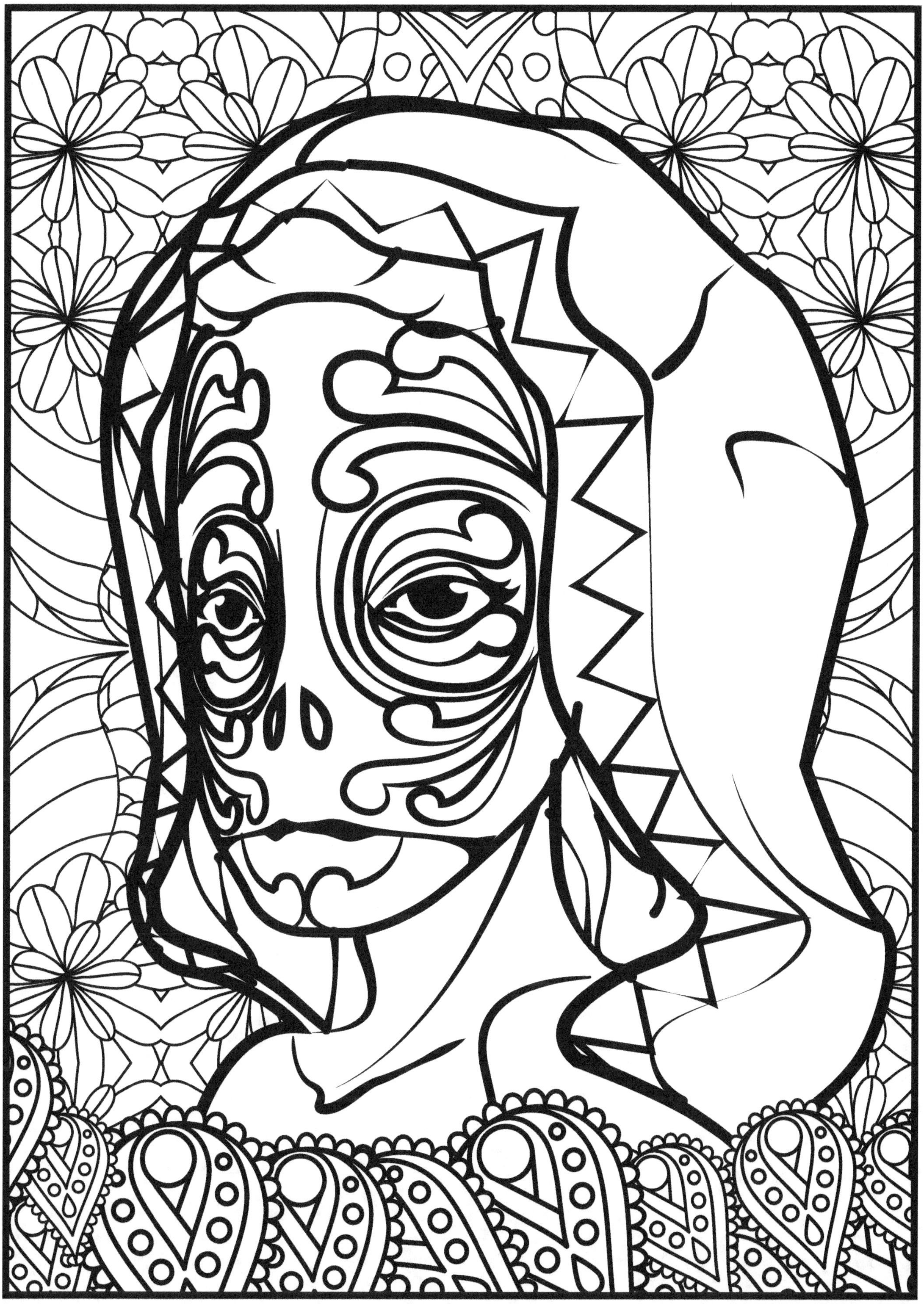

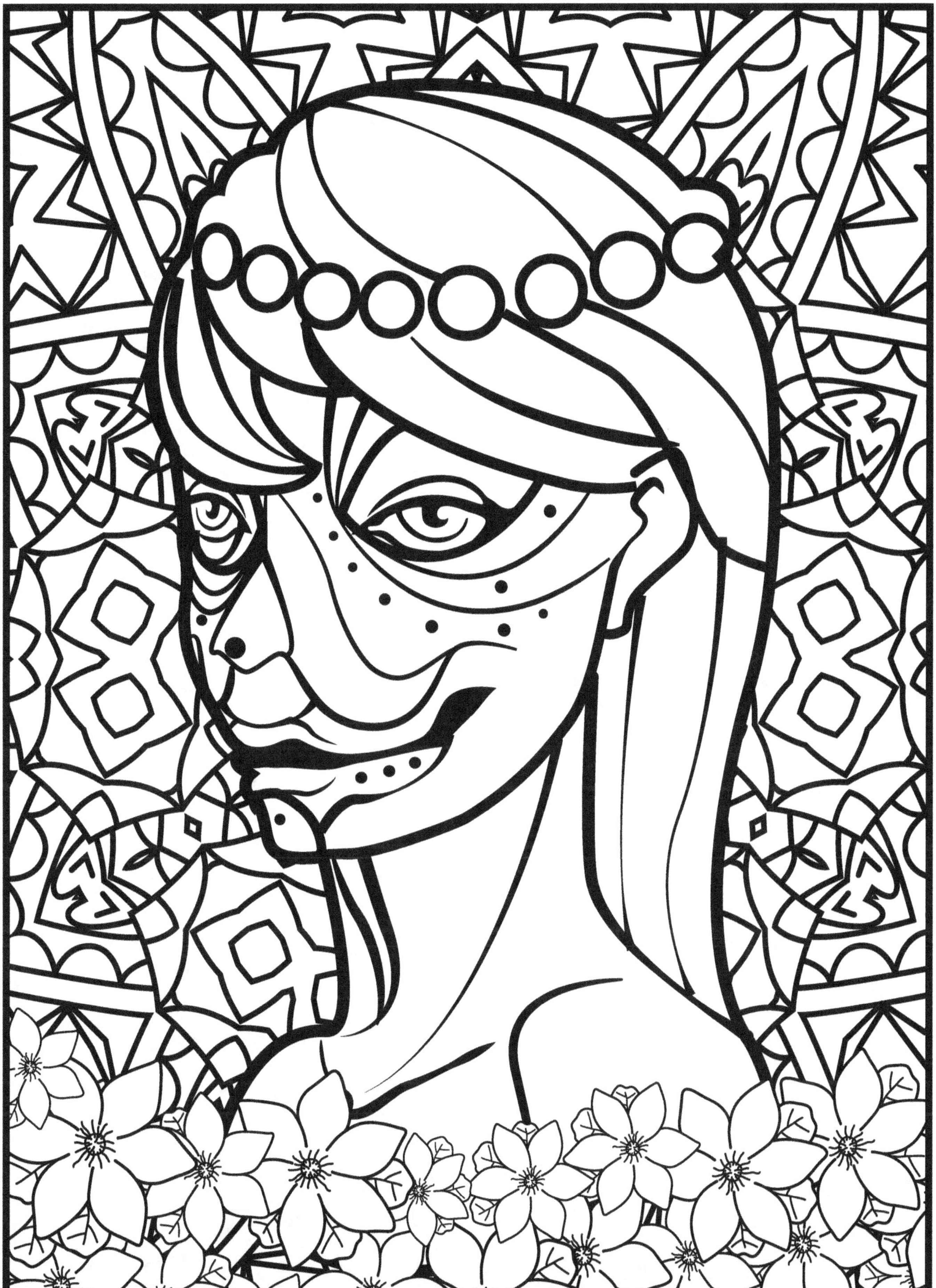

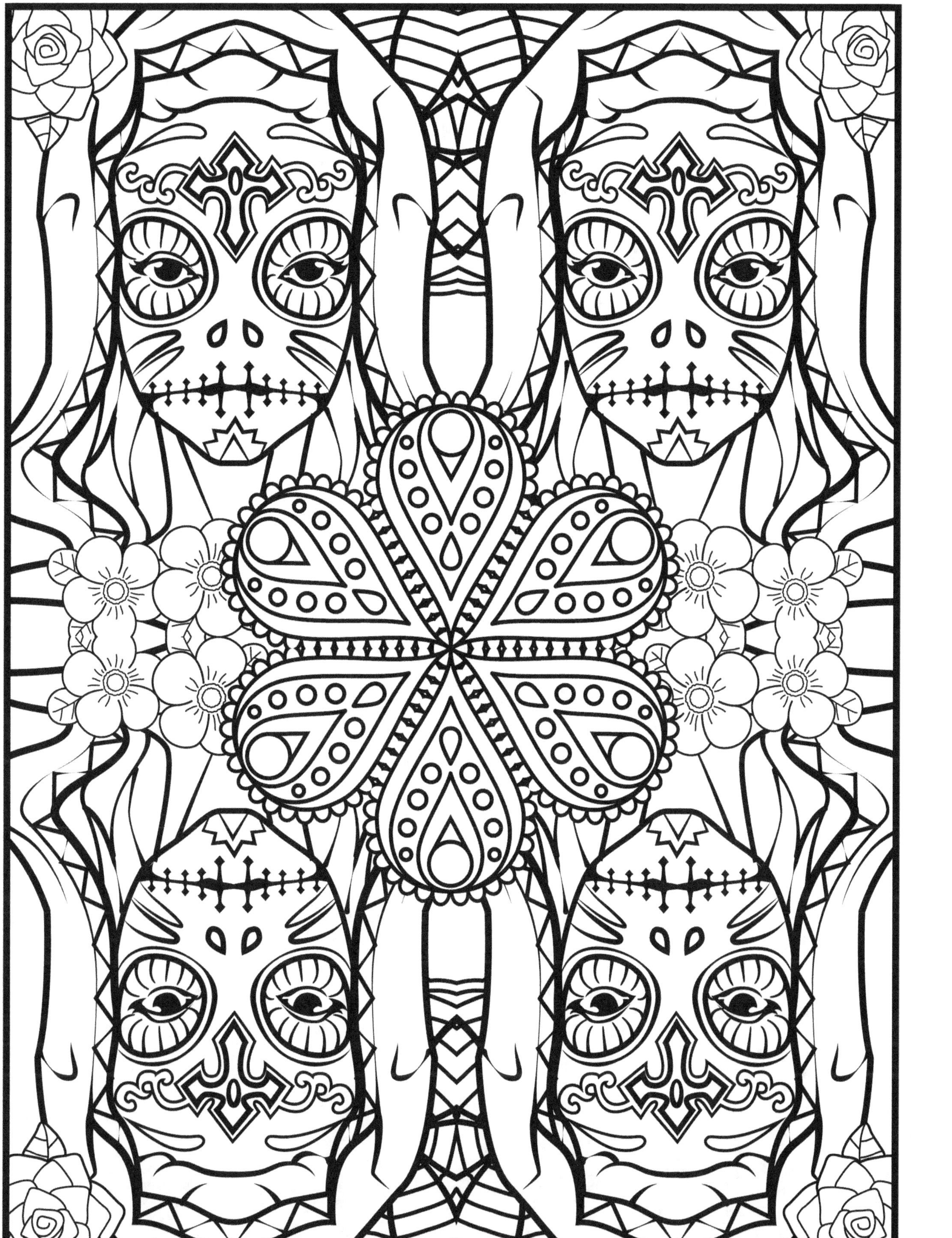

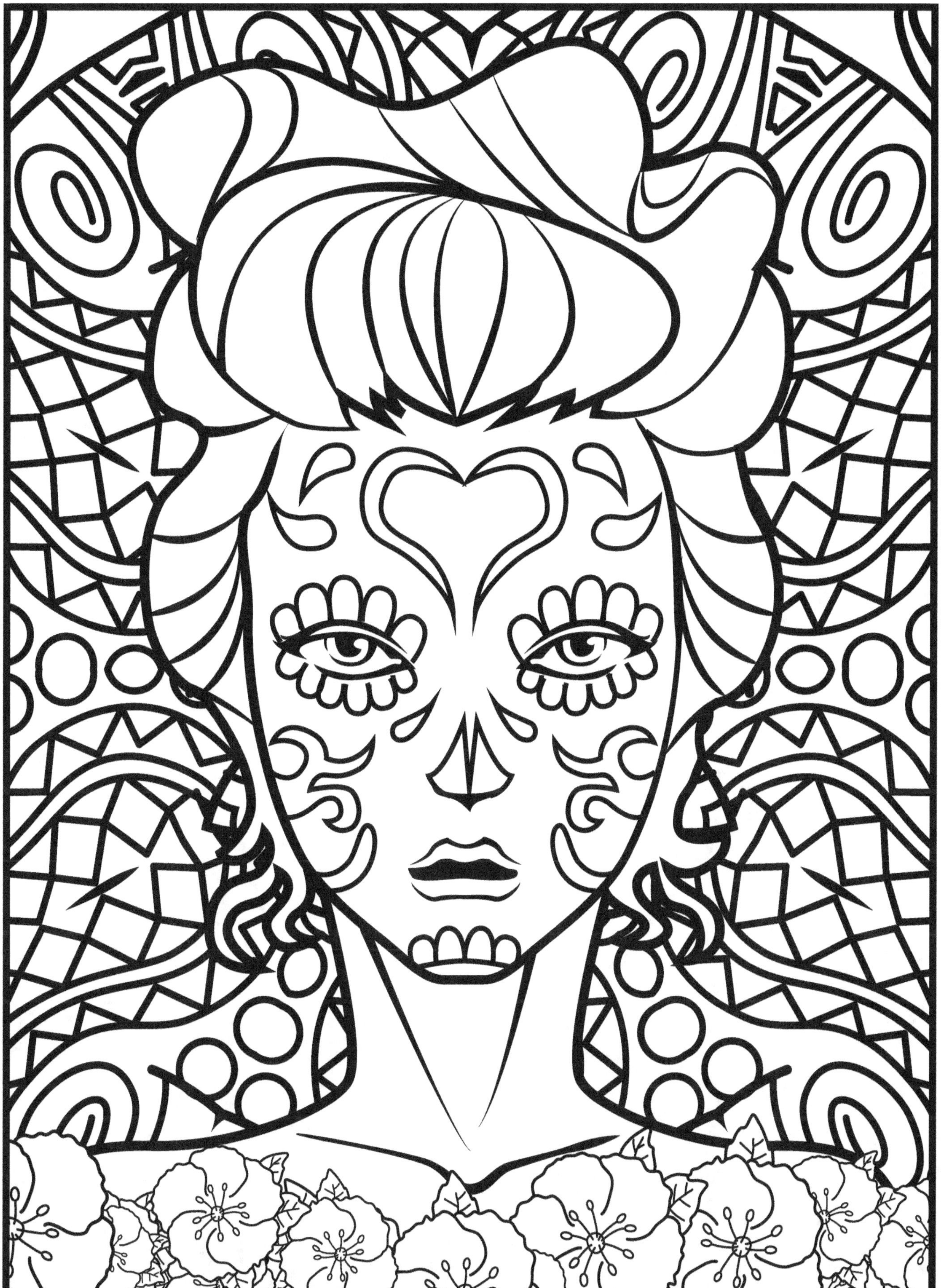

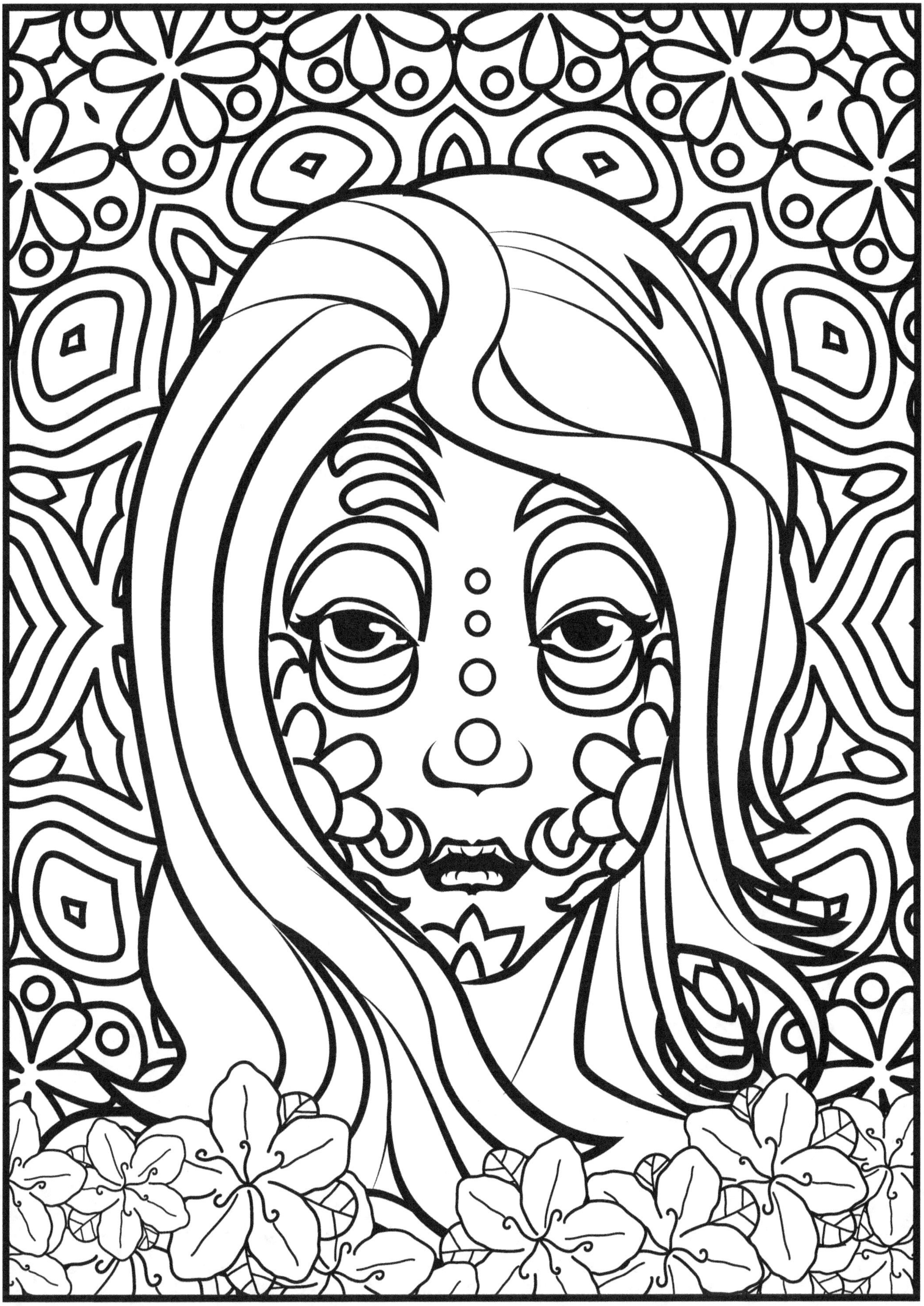

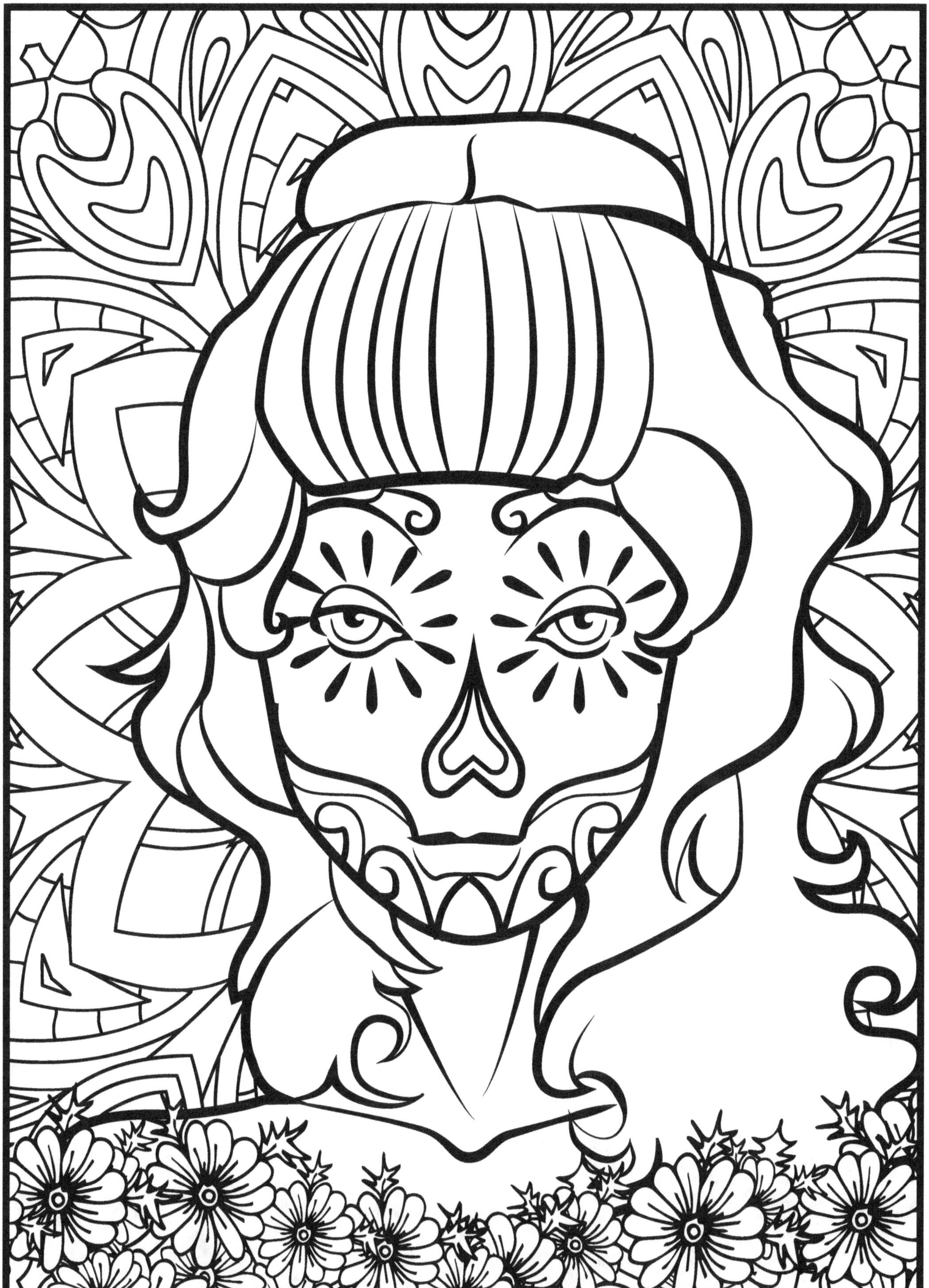

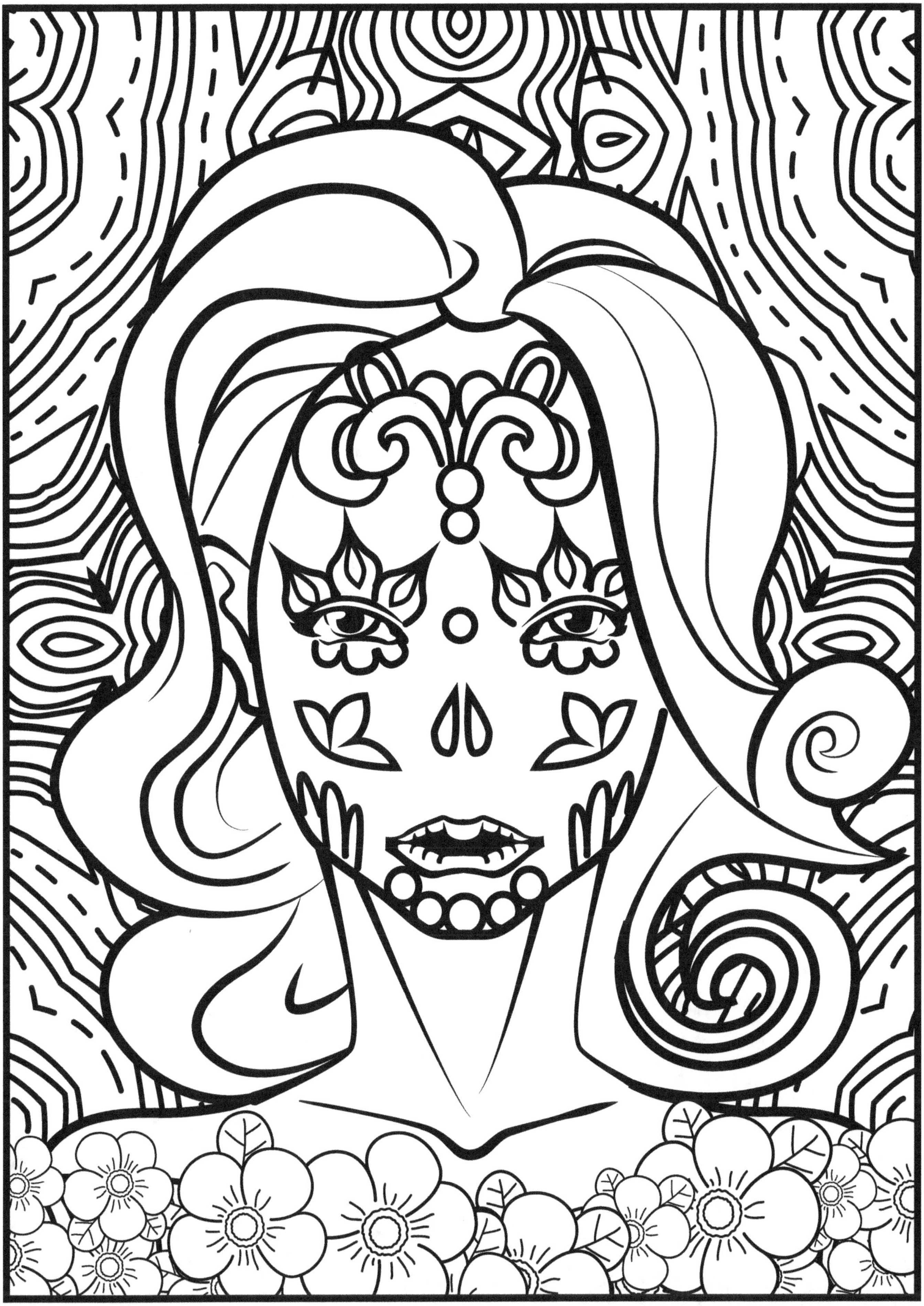

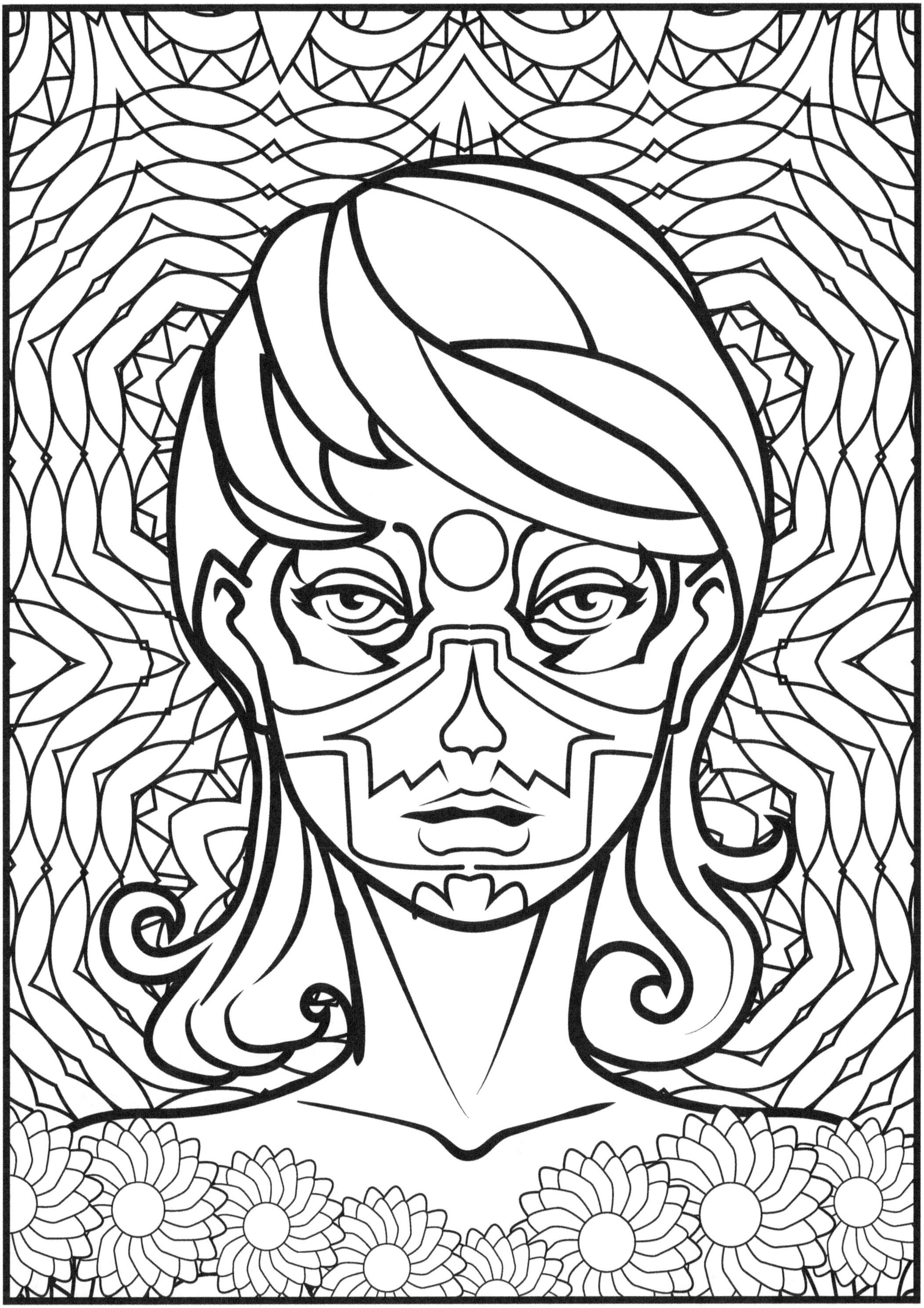

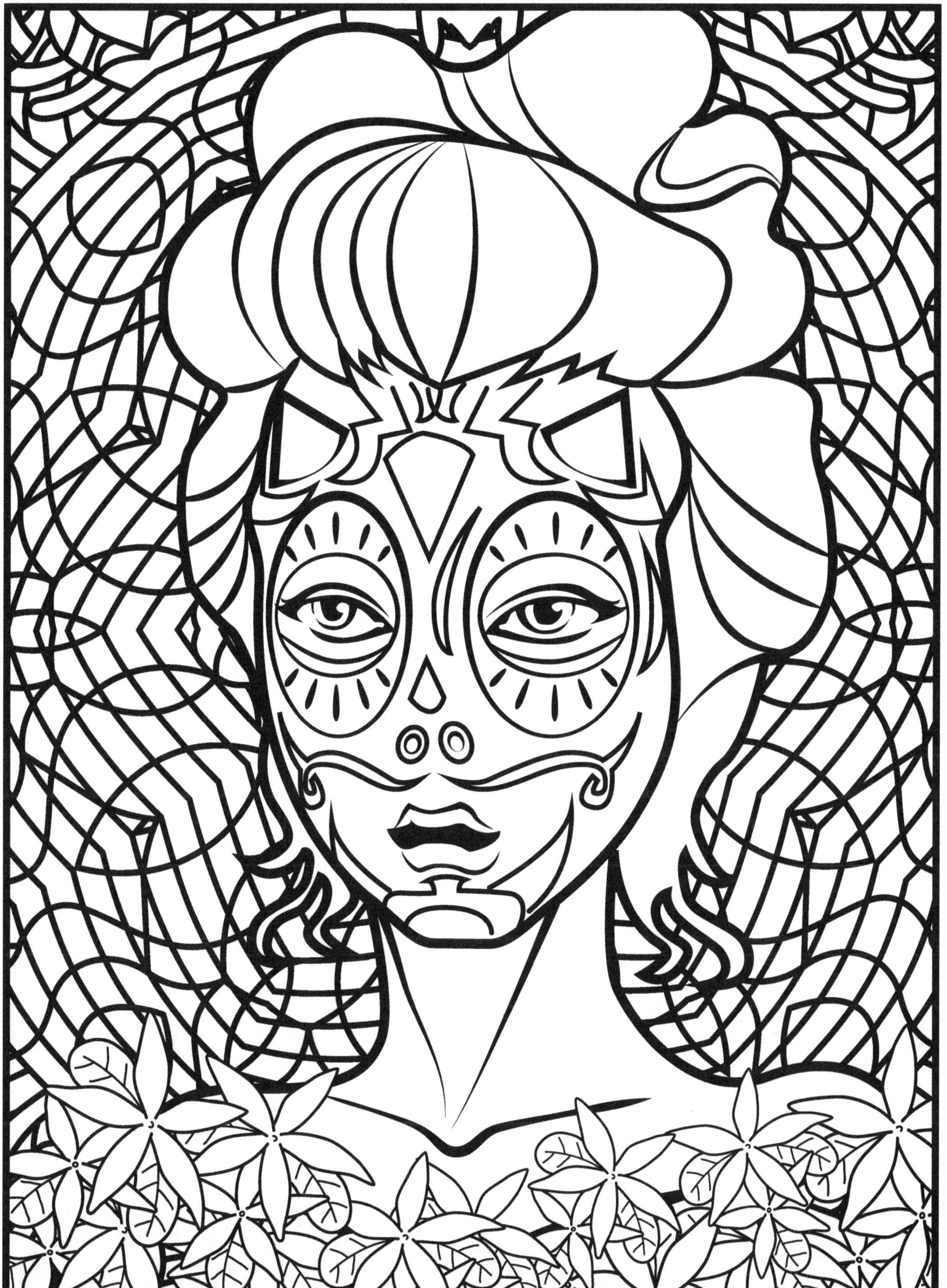

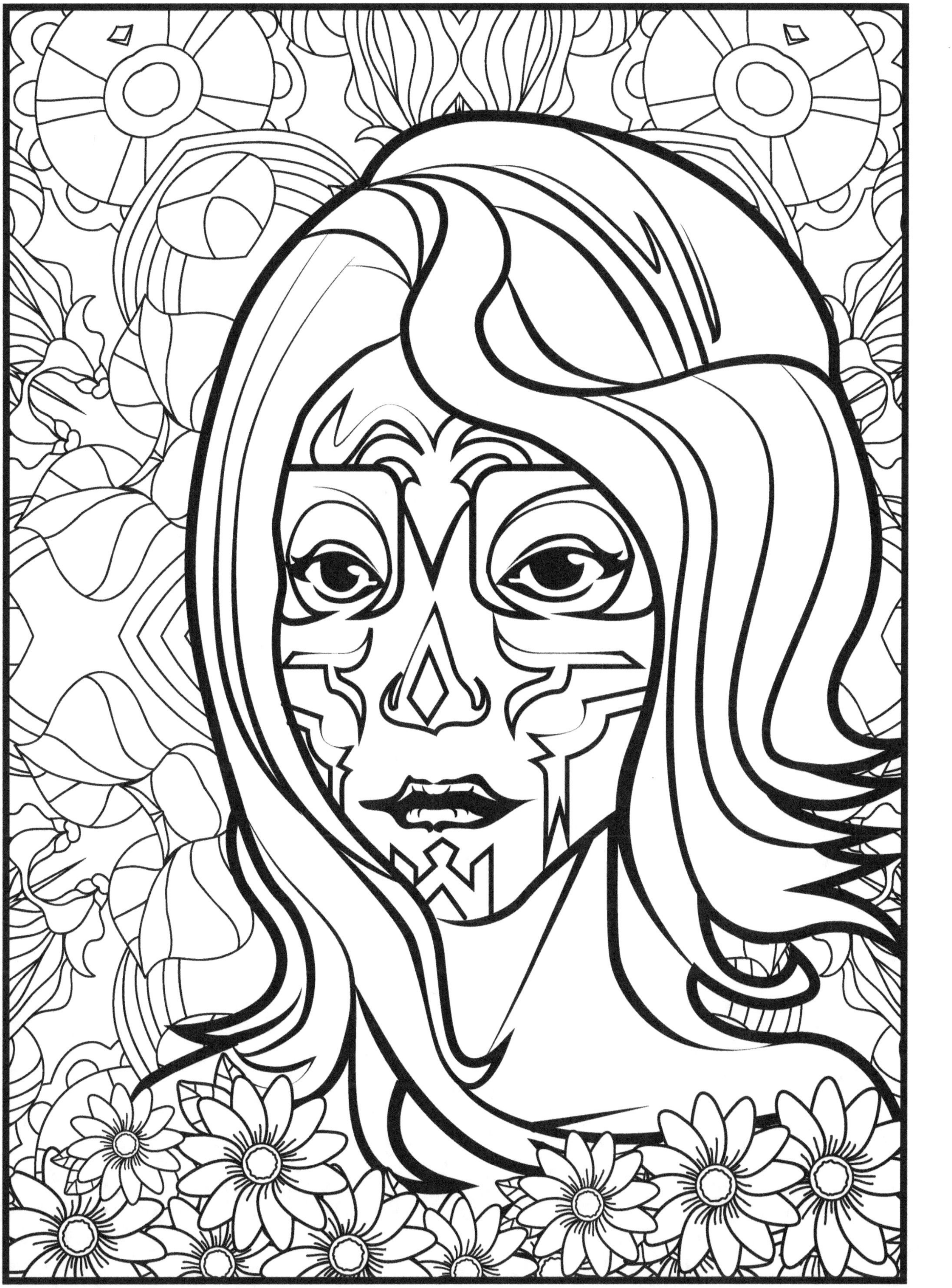

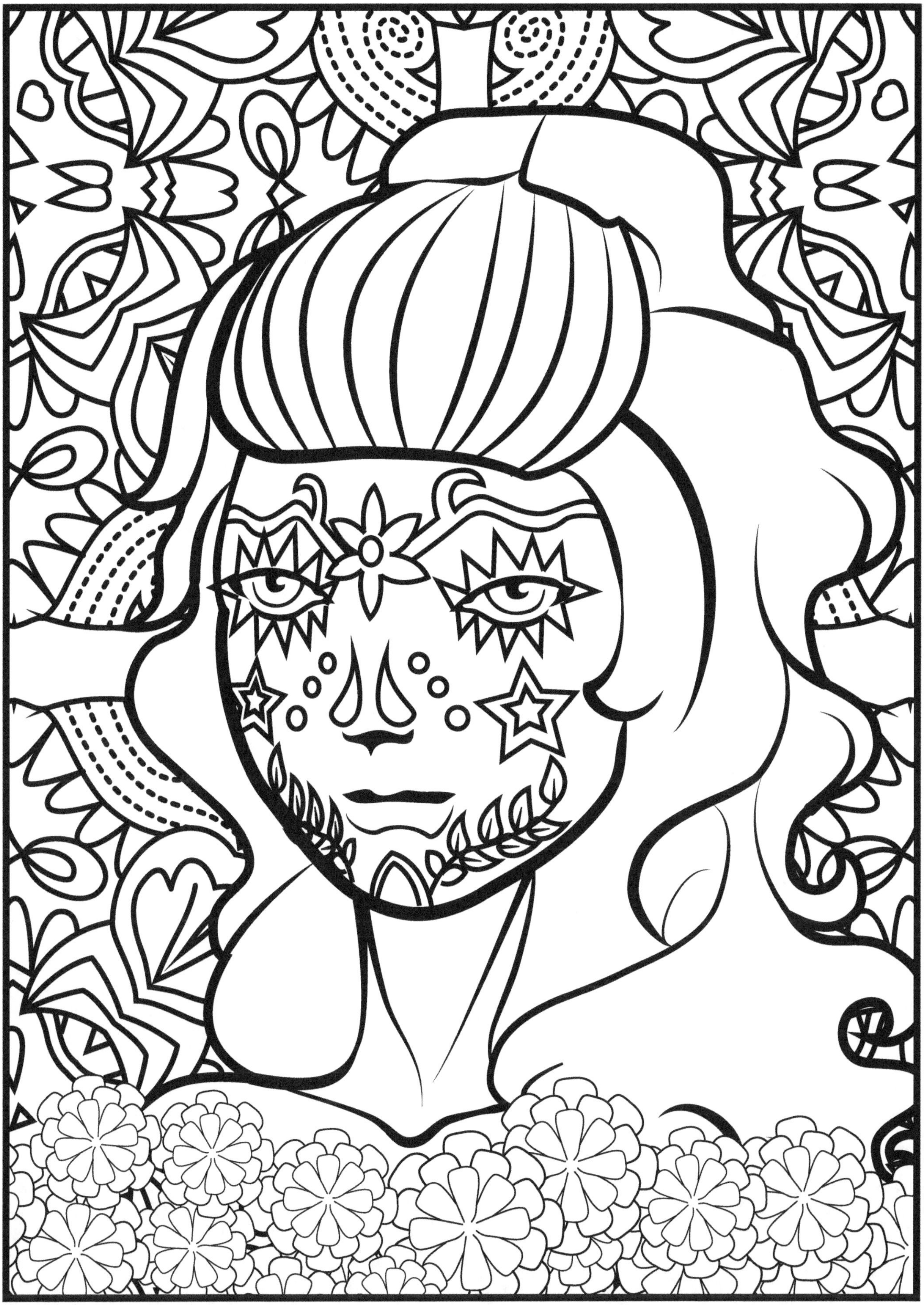

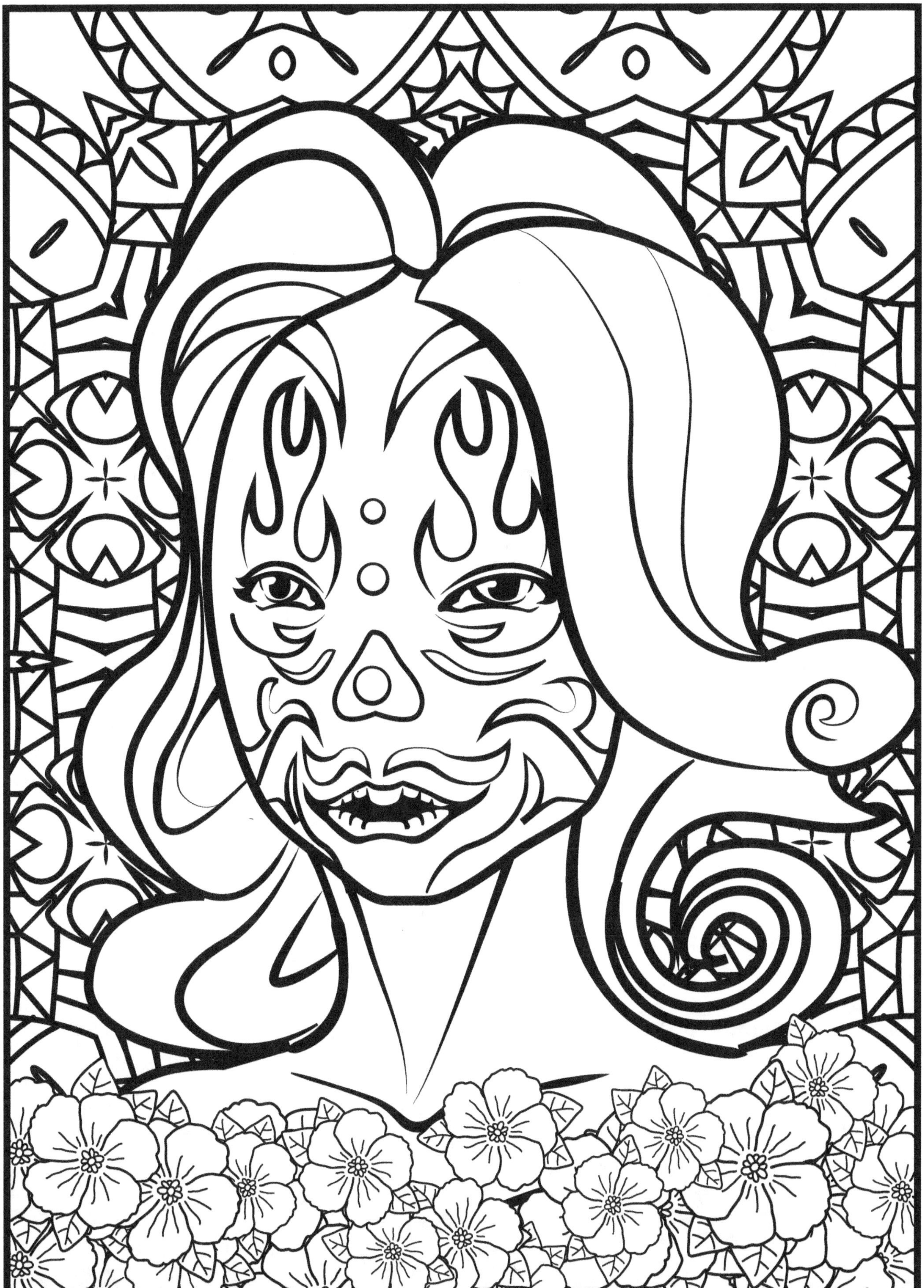

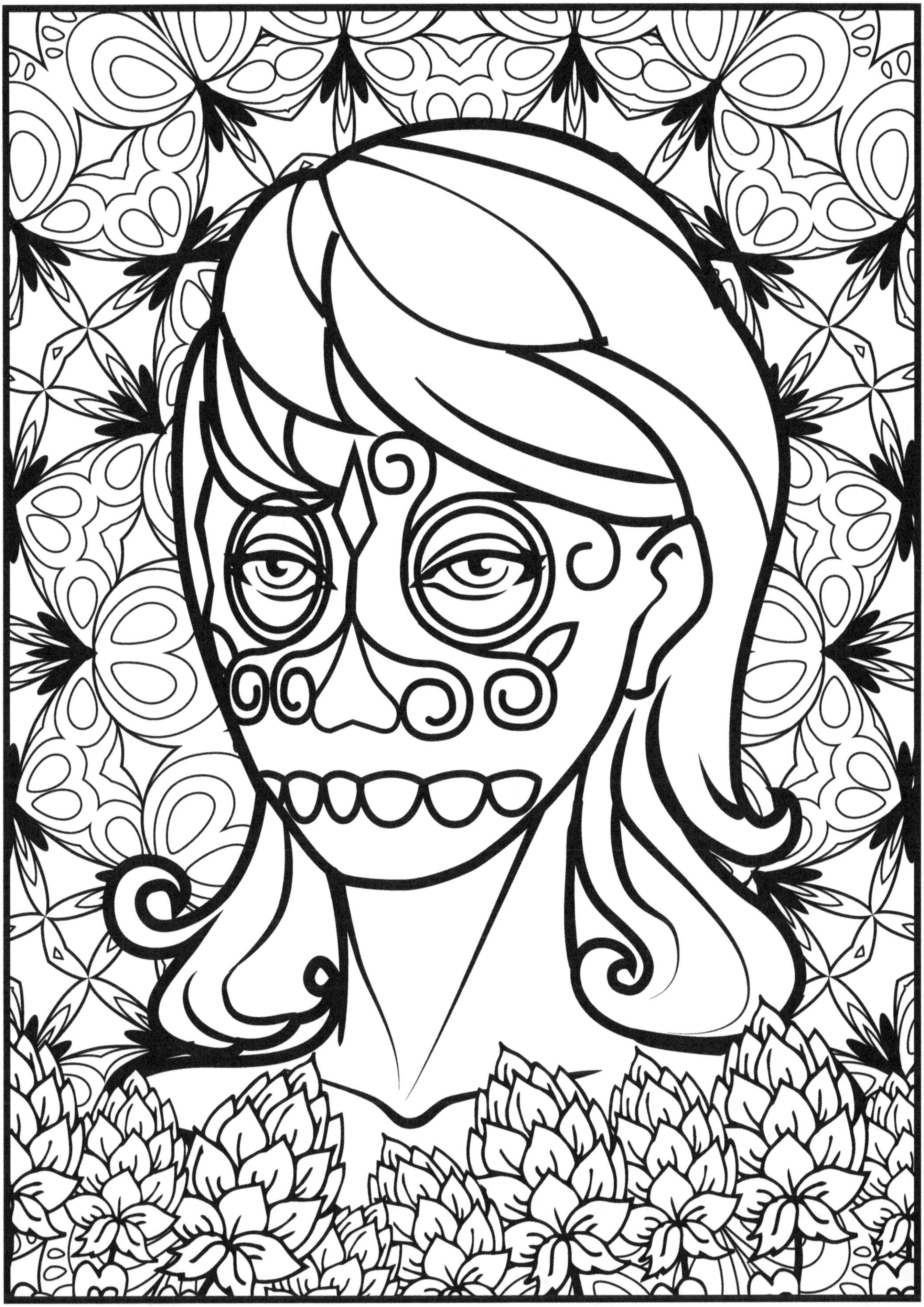

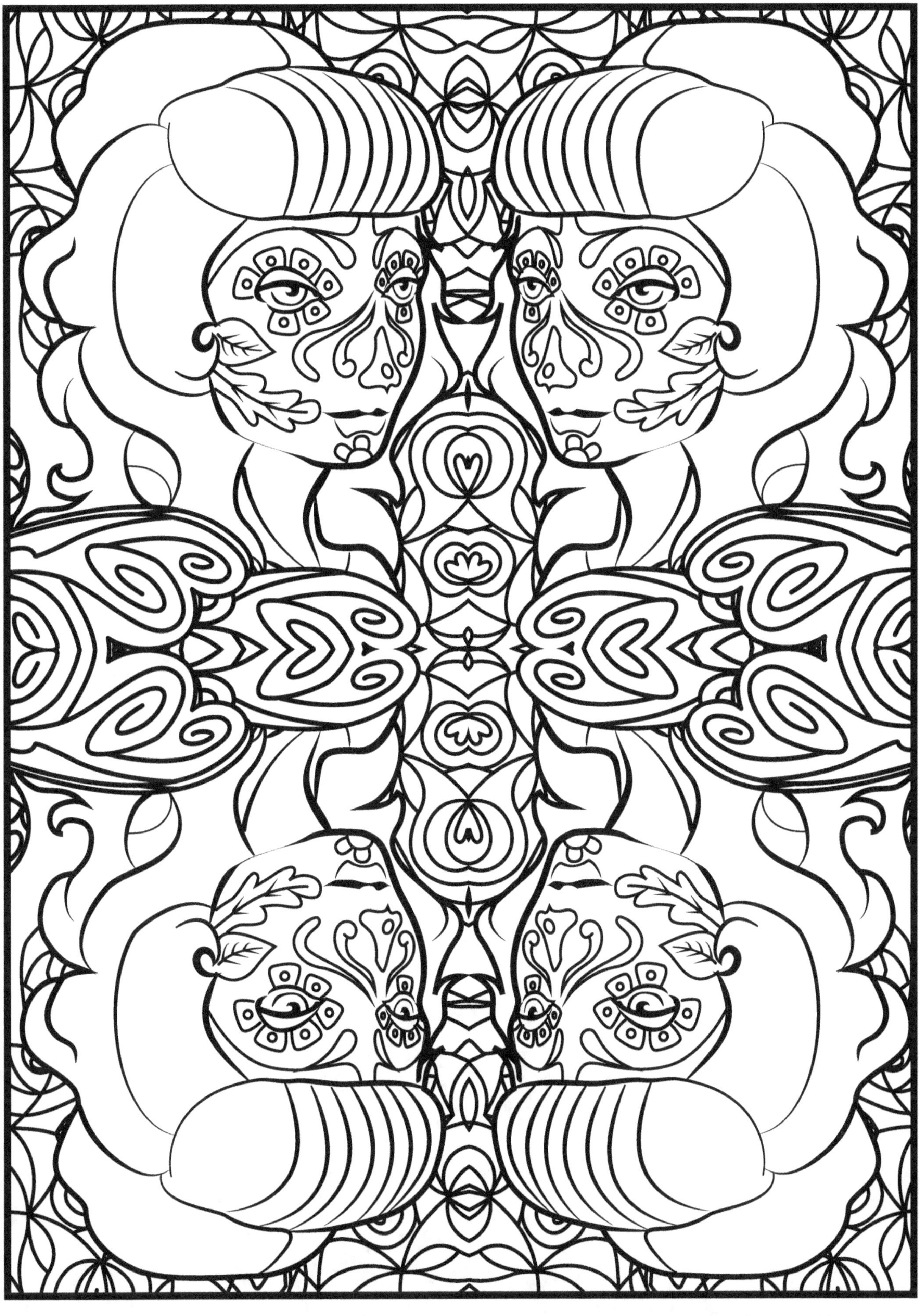

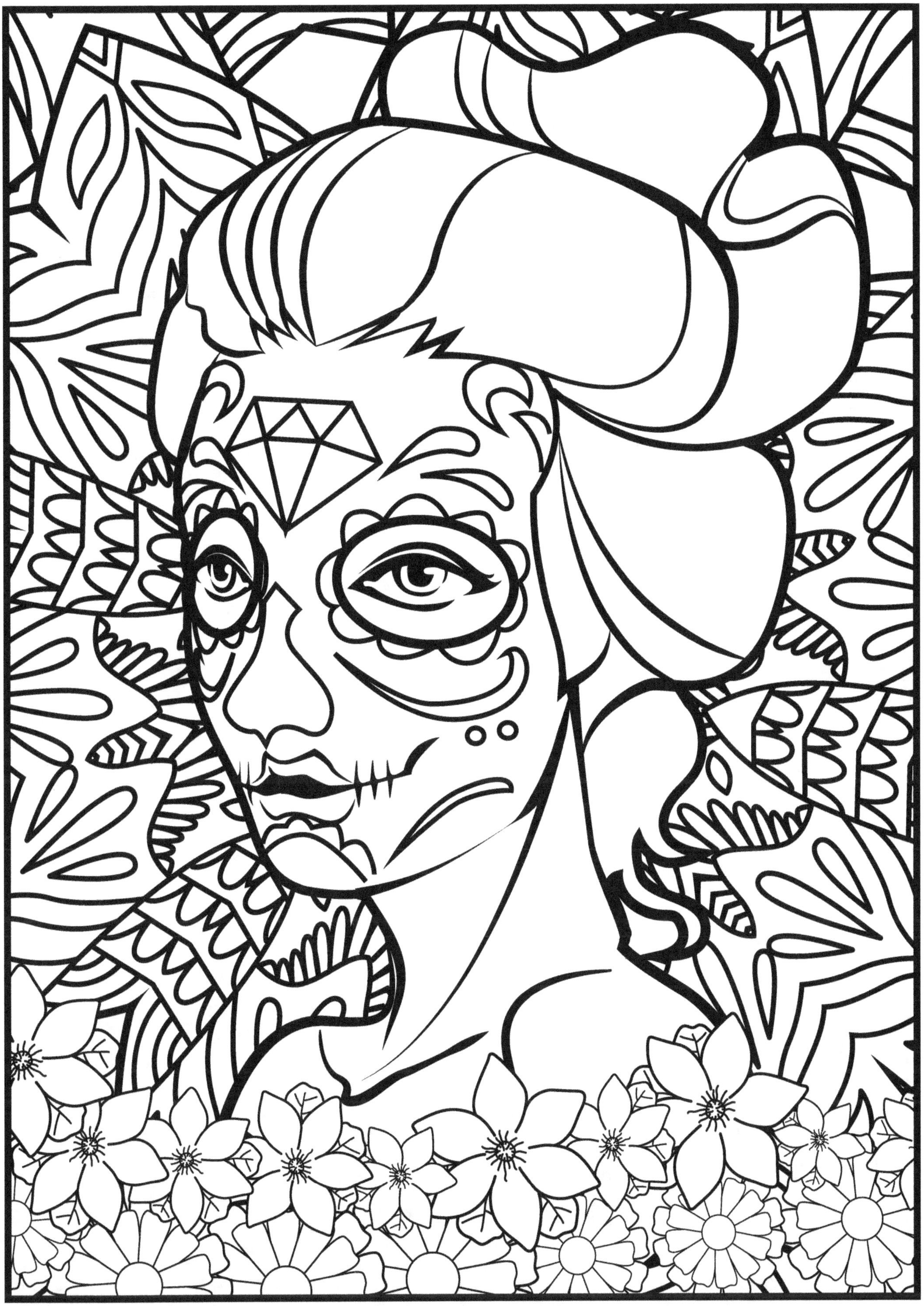

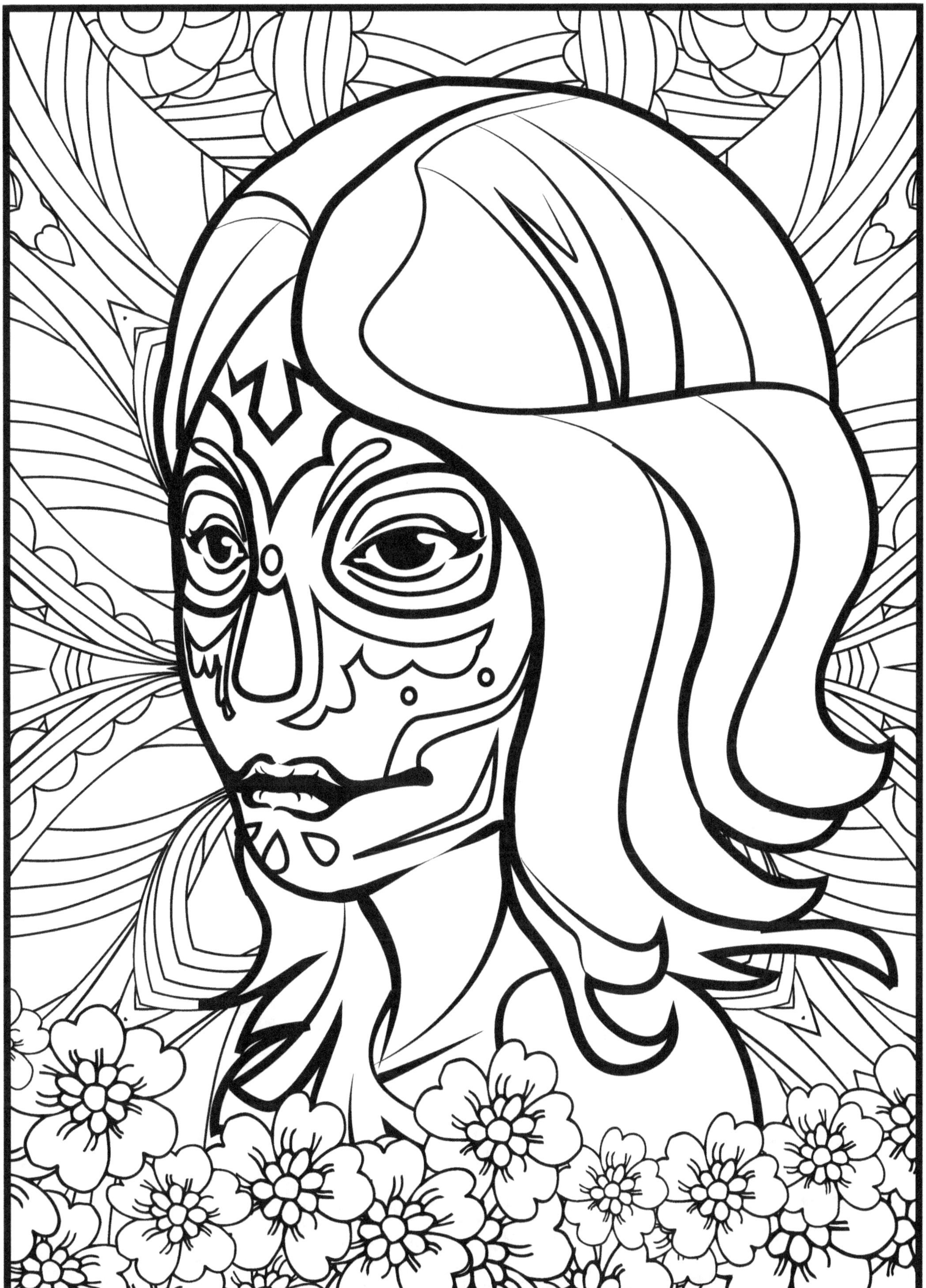

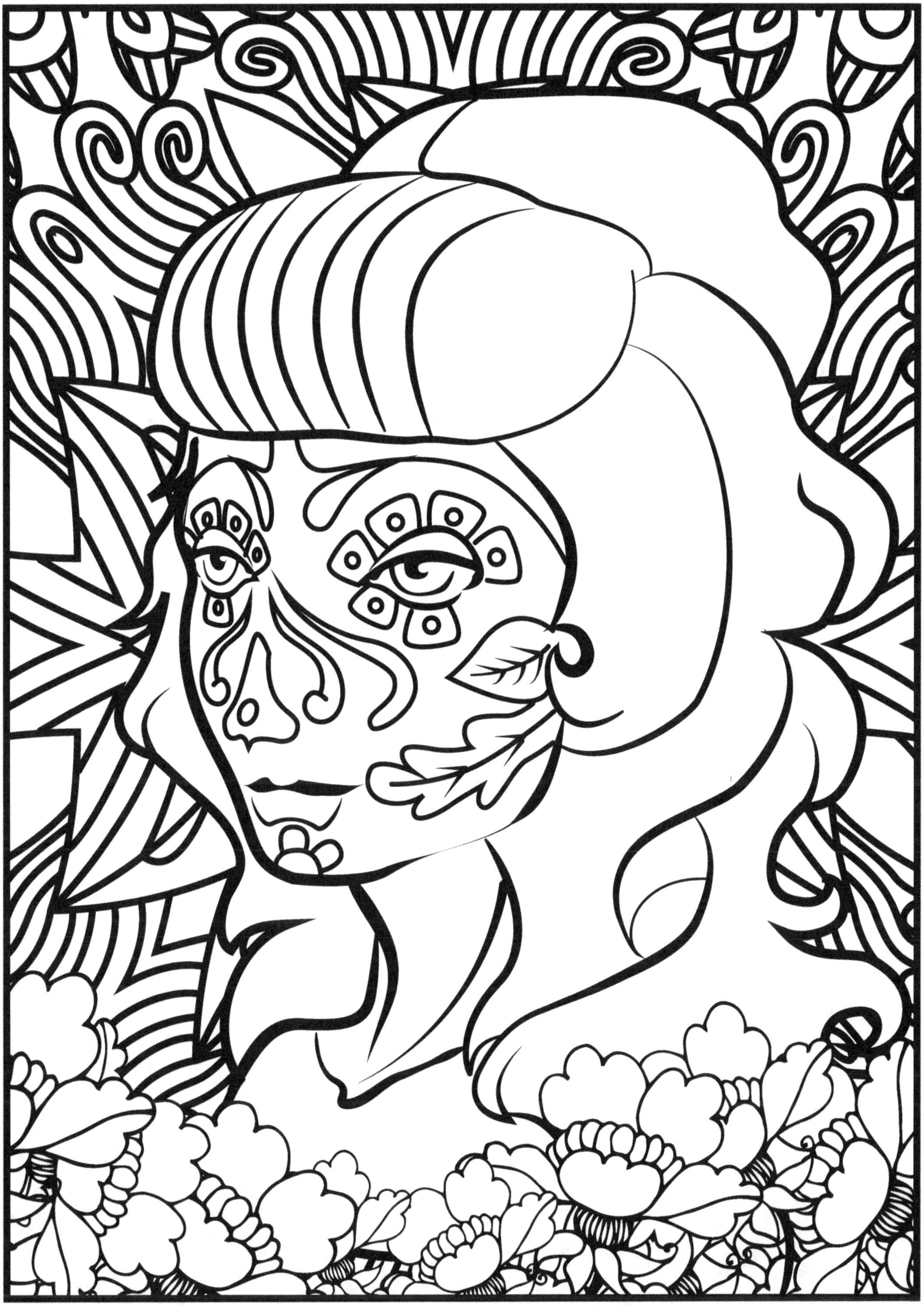

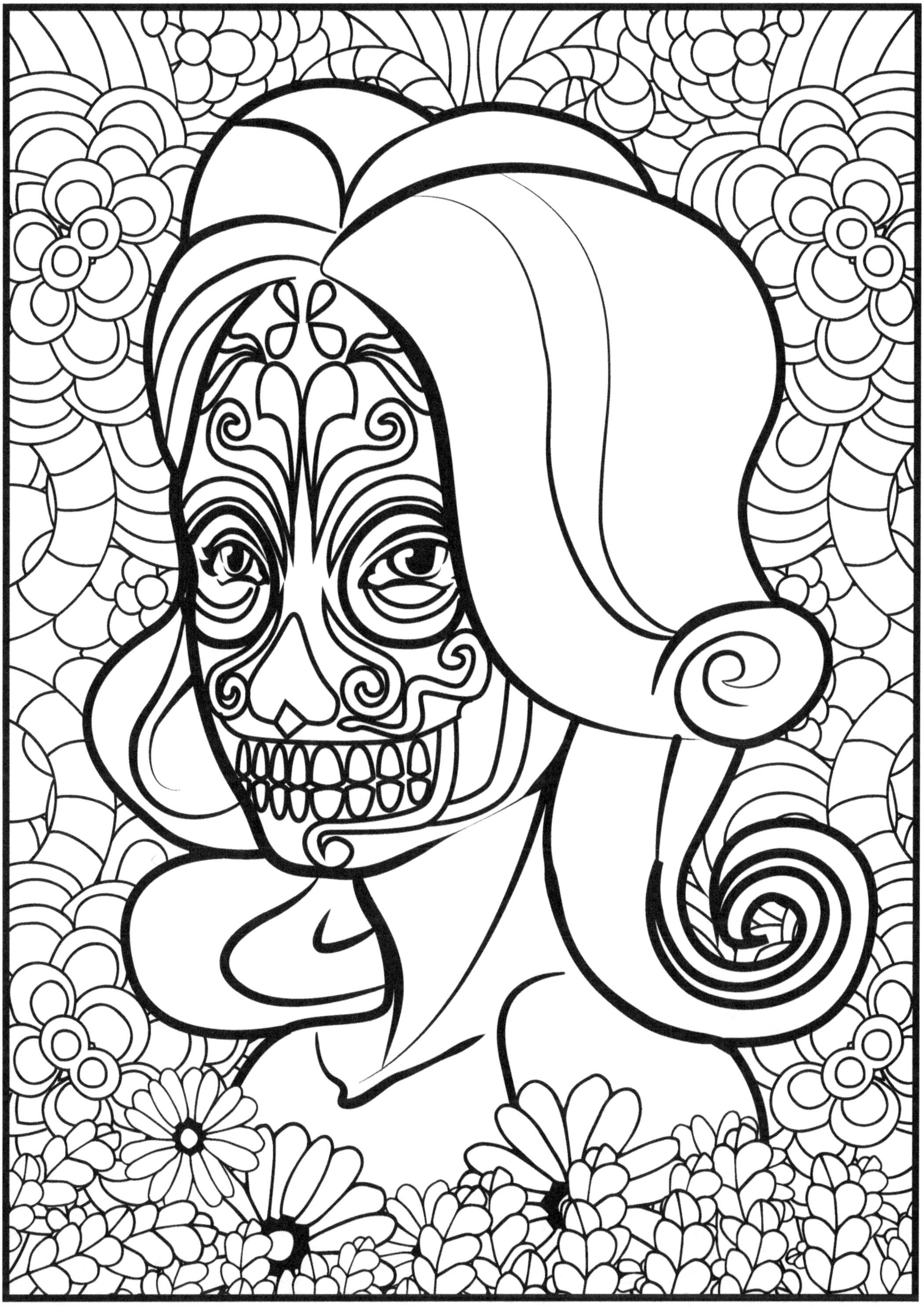

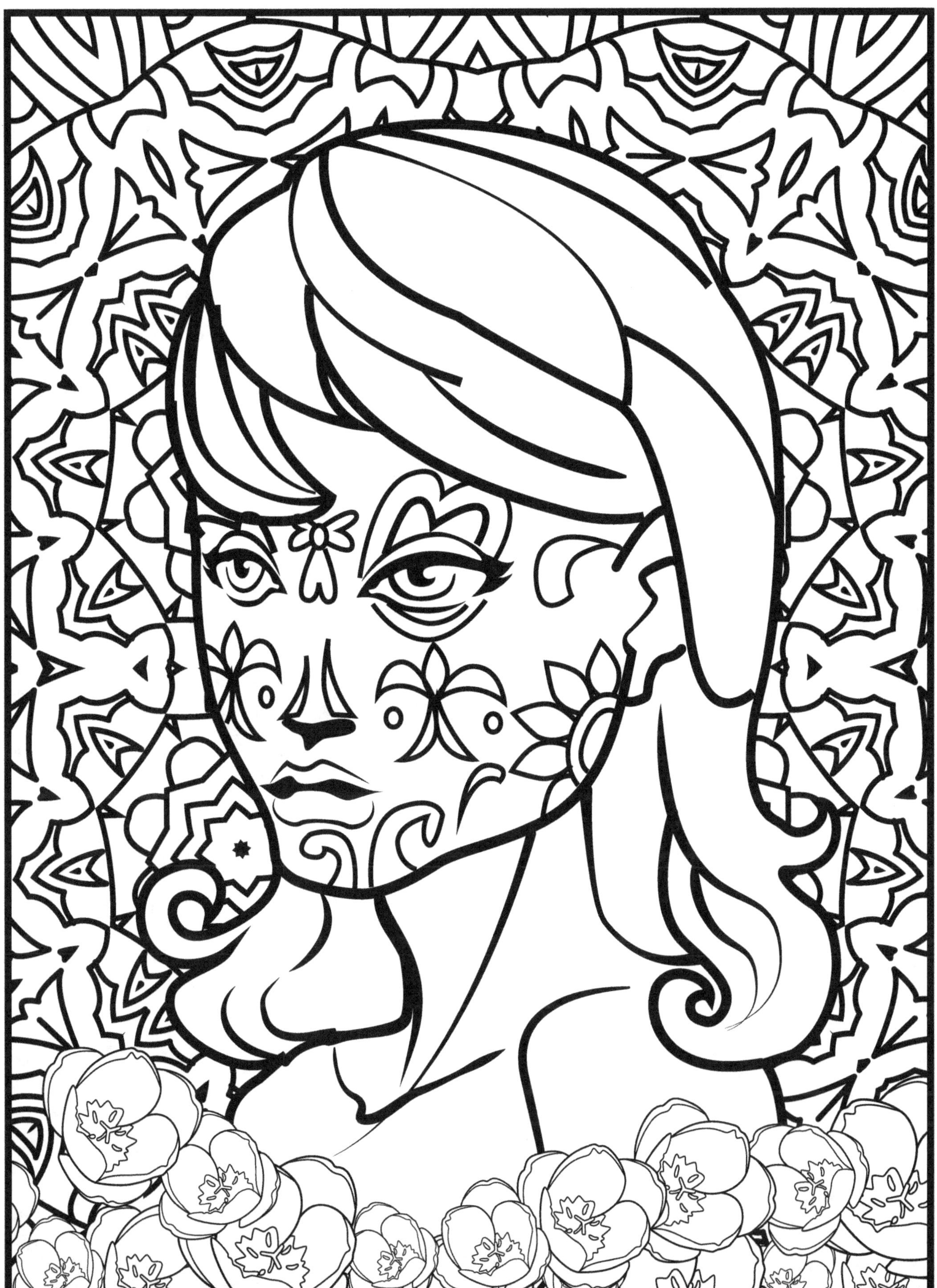

www.ingramcontent.com/pod-product-compliance
Lightning Source LLC
Chambersburg PA
CBHW081311170526
45166CB00011B/3482
9781519337634